Whose Childhood Is It?

The Roles of Children, Adults, and Policy Makers

Richard Eke,
Helen Butcher
and
Mandy Lee

continuum

Continuum International Publishing Group

The Tower Building
11 York Road
London SE1 7NX

80 Maiden Lane
Suite 704
New York NY 10038

www.continuumbooks.com

British Library Cataloguing-in-Publication Data
A catalogue record for this book is available from the British Library.

ISBN: 9780826499813 (paperback)
        9781441173577 (hardcover)

Library of Congress Cataloging-in-Publication Data
Eke, Richard.
Whose childhood is it? : the roles of children, adults, and policy makers/Richard Eke, Helen Butcher and Mandy Lee.
p. cm.
ISBN 978-1-4411-7357-7 (hardback) – ISBN 978-0-8264-9981-3 (pbk.)
1. Child development. 2. Early childhood education. I. Butcher, Helen.
II. Lee, Mandy. III. Title.

LB1101.E54 2009
305.231–dc22   2008047980

Typeset by Newgen Imaging Systems Pvt Ltd, Chennai, India
Printed and bound in Great Britain by CPI Antony Rowe, Chippenham, Wiltshire

Contents

Notes on Contributors

Jane Andrews teaches in a range of areas within Early Childhood Studies and Education Studies and has research interests in children's learning in the home environment and in their language development in particular.

Alison Bailey is a senior lecturer in Geography and Environmental Management and Geography specialist in primary education at the University of the West of England (UWE). She has an interest in how spaces and places are influential in early childhood.

Stephen Barnes has been involved in Education for over 40 years. The main foci of his interests have been Curriculum and Pedagogic Theory, Philosophy, Geography and World Studies.

Helen Butcher is Leader of Early Childhood Provision and Developments at UWE in the School of Education; she has a particular interest in young children's rights.

Richard Eke works at UWE, Bristol, where he is Joint Head of Academic Developments in the Faculty of Social Sciences and Humanities and is Deputy Head of the School of Education. He has an active interest in educational governance and is currently chairman of the National Primary Teacher Education Council. He has a particular interest in young children's engagement with representational forms and learning.

John Lee is Reader in Education and has a long-standing research and professional interest in Early Years provision.

Mandy Lee is a senior lecturer in Education and Early Childhood Studies specializing in children's engagement with contemporary media, at UWE, Bristol.

Sue Norman is a senior lecturer in Early Childhood Studies and Education at UWE with a particular interest in child development and early years policy.

Christine Screech is a senior lecturer in English and Early Years at UWE. She teaches on a range of undergraduate and post-graduate ITE courses and is

Programme Leader for the BA (Hons) early years ITE route. Her particular research interest is in children's transitions in education.

Dr Jane Tarr is director of Training for Children and Young people in the Wider Workforce at the School of Education, UWE, Bristol, and has a research interest in building inclusive school communities that recognize the vital contribution of local communities including parents, families and community members.

Abbreviations and Acronyms

BME	Black and Minority Ethnic
CAF	Common Assessment Framework
CGFS	Curriculum Guidance for the Foundation Stage
CSR	Comprehensive Spending Review
CWDC	Children's Workforce Development Council
CWN	Children's Workforce Network
DCSF	Department for Children, Schools and Families
DFES	Department of Education and Skills
ECEC	Early Childhood Education and Care
ECM	Every Child Matters
EPPE	Effective Provision of Pre-School Education Project
EYFS	Early Years Foundation Stage
EYPS	Early Years Professional Status
NCB	National Children's Bureau
NCH	National Children's Home (now Action for Children)
NESS	National Evaluation of Sure Start
OECD	Organisation for Economic Co-operation and Development
OfSTED	Office for Standards in Education
PLA	Pre-School Learning Alliance
QCA	Qualifications and Curriculum Authority
QTS	Qualified Teacher Status
SSLP	Sure Start Local Programme
TDA	Training and Development Agency for Schools
UNCRC	United Nations Committee on the Rights of the Child

Introduction

The purpose of this book is to promote a thoughtful engagement with key issues and theories that inform our understanding of early childhood. We have framed the book around the challenging question 'Whose Childhood?' in order to provoke questions and invite discussion around the large issues of who determines the shape and boundaries of early childhood and what part children have in this process. As well as examining key issues and theories we also want to talk practically and recognize the possibility that we might allow children space for *their* childhood. The book intends to turn readers away from our collective tendency to simplify the experiences of young children and replace it with a fuller, more complex, more troubling and more realistic understanding of the social dynamic of childhood.

One of the themes that runs through the book, and one which determines many of the responses individuals, agencies and governments have to childhood, is the tension between childhood seen as a place of 'becoming', simply a training ground for adulthood; and the view of childhood as a place of 'being'. We present versions of the view that children are 'beings' whose lives matter now and who are as entitled to Human Rights as the adults they share their lives with. However, children, like adults, are also on a journey and we discuss the extent to which the direction of their journey is dominated by their economic, social and cultural status at birth. Strategies for overcoming structural disadvantage are also raised.

Additionally there are two intertwined themes that permeate this book: first, the impact on children's sense of self of adults' temporal and cultural fabrications of childhood as articulated through policy and provision for young children; secondly, young children and representation, their own representational activity and their struggles to occupy space for playful representation.

In the first part of the book we look at the policies which currently define early childhood in the United Kingdom, England specifically. There are some interesting contradictions in this area, for example, in order for the economy to thrive, the United Kingdom needs a skilled workforce and evidence shows early education impacts on this; so there is an overriding economic imperative pressing on the design and success of early education. We also know that beginning formal education too early is not successful in the long term. However not only do we start children at school earlier than many other countries but it is becoming increasingly formal and subject to regulation and inspection for younger and younger children – from birth in fact.

In the second part of this book we look critically at the opportunity and space for children to be meaning makers in the context of these directives. We question the impact of those directives on the capacity of adults to allow children to make spaces in which their consciousness can flourish. We look at the struggle which children have in order to persist in representing and making sense of their lives. For example, the Early Years Foundation Stage (EYFS) sees early mark making as a literacy activity more than a creative act. This version of children's marks reflects the values and priorities of a 'children as adults in training' model rather than 'beings' engaging in a creative process of their *own*. Provision for young children should, we contend, be about helping them make better sense of their lives rather than eroding their opportunities to do so.

At various points in the book we have, like other critics, cited examples from Italy or New Zealand as providing contrasting examples of engaging with young children in which children are viewed as strong, capable and competent. Much as there is to admire in the educational philosophy of Reggio Emilia and Te Whariki we need to be cautious about simply suggesting that we could borrow policy and import it from one social and cultural context to another. Educational values and beliefs emerge from and mirror societies more often than leading the way, and so we should reflect on what current early education tells us about our society and culture: specifically about visions of childhoods. However, inspirational practices gathered from around the world, and locally, can point us towards richer understandings of children and childhoods than are currently evidenced in national proposals.

This book has been written by a group of academics who have contributed to the success of the undergraduate and post graduate Early Childhood programmes at UWE. From a range of backgrounds and interests including children's rights, special educational needs, interactive technology, social geography and children's symbolic representation, all have worked professionally with young children as well as alongside colleagues implementing curricula and social policies. We are grateful to colleagues both in early years settings and at UWE for sharing their insights and understandings with us although of course any errors of fact or omission are entirely ours. Together we have worked towards a social vision of childhoods which is gathered here for anyone whose engagement with young children causes them to think about questions which we find endlessly fascinating: what is childhood and who is it for?

Part I
POLICY AND CHILDHOOD

Introduction

In this section of the book you will find that four key policy documents are critiqued. These are: The United Nations Convention on the Rights of the Child (UNCRC) (1989), Every Child Matters (2003), Early Years Foundation Stage (2007) and The Children's Plan (2007).

We begin with a chapter on Sure Start by Sue Norman because it encapsulates so many aspects of early childhood policy and its reach into provision in the United Kingdom, in particular in England. Sue shows us how policy-makers first drew on research in framing the provision and then ignored it when it did not match their policy requirements. She chronicles the role of the Treasury in these developments and the shortcomings of an underfinanced shift away from provision targeted on the socially excluded to universal provision.

In Chapter 2 Jane Andrews and Helen Butcher offer a critical analysis of policies and their consequences in terms of target-driven provision. They focus on the impact of a fierce regulatory structure on children and their families. The chapter includes a discussion of the development of educare and the tensions between state and family and raises issues about the manner in which an outcomes driven approach bear down on both of these. The authors contrast such an approach with a consideration of the why and how of consulting with children and include an example, drawn from their empirical data, of very young children's participation.

In Chapter 3 Christine Screech develops an analysis that highlights the creeping curricularization of early childhood. Starting with the Plowden Report and moving through the Education Reform Act and later curriculum proposals for the foundation stage and Birth to 3 Matters, Christine concludes with a discussion of the statutory arrangements and EYFS. She highlights tensions between curriculum arrangements and spontaneity and draws attention to alternative arrangements.

In Chapter 4 Jane Tarr asks about policy initiatives that encourage young children's capacity to realize their rights and responsibilities. Jane identifies the consistent failure of UK governments to fully implement the UNCRC. She argues that all professionals working with young children in early years settings need training in order to enable them to ensure that children are respected and know their entitlements. Children need to be able to actively participate in all things that enhance their own lives and learning.

This first part of the book is intended to provide a rich engagement with the large scale policy agendas that impact on early childhood provision.

Give Sure Start a Fair Start

Sue Norman

1

Chapter Outline

This chapter examines the historical and political context and the original aims of Sure Start, then looks at the factors that have led to changes in Sure Start and considers whether this has led to the disappearance of the programme or simply a political re-branding. Research findings by the National Evaluation of Sure Start (NESS) team and the difficulties of drawing any firm conclusions about the success or failure of Sure Start will also be discussed. You will be asked to reflect on the consequence of this policy for children in terms of whether they are central in policy formation and to what extent their needs are being met.

Key Questions

1. What is Sure Start and what challenges is it trying to address?
2. What is the wider policy context surrounding the Sure Start agenda?
3. Does Sure Start give a good start to life?
4. How does the approach position children?

A number of key policies and events are referred to in this chapter. We begin with a table summarizing these for easy reference.

Key policies

Date	Policy	Comment
1989	United Nations Convention on the Rights of the Child ratified	States that children have the right to be protected from illness and neglect, receive an education, be protected from abuse and to be listened to. Legal framework for this in the United Kingdom is provided primarily by the Children Acts of 1989 and 2004. The convention stated that there should be an increasing transfer of decision making to the child as the child gets older.
1989	Children Act	Legal framework for UNCRC. Also included non-statutory guidance for education in the Early Years supported by Local Authority inspections.
1990	*Starting with Quality* (the Rumbold Report) published	An enquiry into the quality of education for under-5s. Stated that those working with under-5s must recognize the importance of their educational role and highlighted the importance of preparing children for the National Curriculum.
1992	OfSTED (Office for Standards in Education) set up	This provided for the inspection of the educational provision for children of compulsory school age.
1997	New Deal for lone parents	Part of the aim to move people from welfare to work. Included a commitment by the government to provide accessible and affordable childcare.
1997	National Children's Bureau published an independent paper, 'Quality in Diversity in Early Learning: A Framework for Early Childhood practitioners'.	Argued that quality judgements about early childhood settings need to be able to deal with diverse contexts.
1998	DfEE National Childcare Strategy	Proposed setting up 25 Early Excellence Centres to provide childcare, education and a neighbourhood nursery programme and free part-time nursery places for all 4-year-olds
1998	Green Paper 'Meeting the Childcare Challenge' published	Recommended extending free part time nursery education to 3-year-olds and transferring responsibility from Health to DfEE.
July 1998	Comprehensive Spending Review	Included a review of services for young children with particular interest in the benefits of early intervention. £540m spend on young children.

July 1998	Sure Start programme announced	The first two projects began in October 1999 – with the central aim of eradicating child poverty by 2020. About 250 programmes aimed at outreach, support, childcare, community health care and support for special needs, based in areas of deprivation but open to everyone in the area. Emphasis on parental involvement; however, also involved the government having some input into bringing up children, so shifting some of the responsibility away from parents.
July 2000	Decision to expand the Sure Start programme to 550 projects	Decision taken despite lack of evidence that they were meeting their aims.
2001	Local authorities assumed responsibility for support services.	Early Years providers were expected to provide education as well as care; so, responsibility for Early years was transferred from Health to Education. The educational provision was to be inspected by OfSTED and an Early Years directorate was set up.
2001	Curriculum Guidance for the Foundation Stage published.	Guidance provided was very specific but still non-statutory.
2002	Birth to Three Matters published.	Intended to improve the quality of provision for 0–3 although some were concerned with legislating for the experiences of the youngest children.
November 2002	The Childcare Review	These would be based on the lessons learned from Sure Start; proposed the idea of Children's Centres.
2003	The Green Paper *Every Child Matters* published and the Children Act 2004 passed, giving legal status to the outcomes	Followed the report by Lord Laming into the murder of Victoria Climbie. Established five aims for all children: Be healthy, stay safe, enjoy and achieve, make a positive contribution and achieve economic wellbeing. The Children Act also prioritized children on the policy agenda – the post of a Children's Commissioner, a Minister for Children and the creation of Children's Trusts in all local authorities to integrate all child and family services locally.
2003	Children's Centres were to be established in every local authority ward as part of the Sure Start programme	The most deprived 20% of wards would get a centre first. They were intended to be one-stop centres for children under 5 and their families. Neighbourhood Nurseries Initiative and Early Excellence Centres also part of Sure Start.
2003	Excellence and Enjoyment: National Primary Strategy published	Included plans for schools to work in partnership with parents and the community as well as proposing that schools extend their services to provide 'wrap-around care' from 8 a.m. to 6 p.m.

⇨

2004	Government launched a ten-year childcare strategy	Based on research findings from the EPPE project.
2004	Comprehensive Spending Review	Announced that there would be 2,500 Children's Centres open by 2008 and 3,500 by 2010.
2005	Sure Start Local Programmes (SSLPs) functioning as Children's Centres – placed under local authority control by 2006	Children's Centres less well resourced than SSLPs.
2005	The Children's Workforce Strategy (DfES 2005) published	Aimed at increasing the skills of those who are not teachers who are working in pre-school settings. Based on the EPPE study findings that better pre-school settings had better qualified staff. The Children's Workforce Development Council (CWDC) was created to oversee this.
2006	Childcare Act 2006	Introduced new legal duties for Local Authorities to improve outcomes for under-5s and promoted childcare provision via Children's Centres and Extended Schools. The Act introduced a duty to implement the new *Early Years Foundation Stage* from 2008, thus removing the distinction between early education and childcare for under 5s.
2007	Early Years Professional Status (EYPS) offered by accredited providers	Based on the findings of the EPPE project and overseen by the CWDC. Standards for the qualification include addressing and assessing children based on the EYFS. Aims to have someone with EYPS in all children's centres by 2010 and in every daycare centre by 2015.
2007	Report by UNICEF on childhood in industrialized nations based on data from 2000 to 2003	Resulting league table put the United Kingdom at the bottom out of 21 countries.
2007	Creation of the new Department for Children, Schools and Families (DCSF)	Responsible for all issues affecting children up to the age of 19.
2007	Children's Plan published	Aiming to improve children's lives in this country, with goals for 2010 and 2020. Based on five principles: support for parents and families, encourage children's potential, enjoyment of childhood, services should be responsive, prevention is better than tackling the results of failure.
2008	*Early Years Foundation Stage* established – part of the 2006 Childcare Act	This new curriculum removed the distinction between early education and childcare for under-5s.
2008	Children's commissioners report to the UN	Reported widespread infringements of the human rights of children as outlined in the UNCR (1989). The Commissioners criticized the government for not targeting the children who are at greatest risk.

⇨

| 2008 | Budget Paper: Ending child poverty – everybody's business | Announcement of a series of measures to tackle child poverty and increase social mobility. Includes the Child Development Grant of around £200 available to low-income parents of children up to the age of 5. Parents will only be eligible if they take agreed actions to support their children's development. |
| | | 30 new Children's Centres will be set up across 10 local Authorities to support parents in finding and progressing in work. |

What is Sure Start and what challenges is it trying to address?

Sure Start is a radical cross-departmental strategy to raise the physical, social, emotional and intellectual status of young children through improved services. It is targeted at children under 4 years of age and their families in areas of need.

(Glass 1999, p. 257)

It was set up as a cornerstone of the UK government's drive to tackle child poverty and social exclusion since levels of child poverty in the United Kingdom are high by European standards (Rutter 2006). A key difference between this and other UK interventions is that programmes were area based and therefore open to *all* children under 4 and their families within these areas. This was intended to reduce any stigma associated with accessing the provision (Belsky et al. 2007). The original programme was established in 1998 with £540 million of government funding to provide 250 local programmes covering 150,000 children (Pugh 2006). As we shall see, the design of the Sure Start programme was heavily influenced by early intervention programmes that were set up in the United States nearly 40 years previously.

Why did the government set up Sure Start?

The government was trying to address the issues of poverty and social exclusion through making an early intervention into children's lives via the Sure

Start programme. During the 1980s and early 1990s the prevailing political view was that it was parents who were responsible for their children (Pugh 2006). However, research findings from the United States showing the long-term benefits of pre-school intervention programmes that had been running for more than 30 years began to renew interest in pre-school intervention in the United Kingdom (Weinberger et al. 2005). The implementation of such programmes led to a shift in the perceived responsibility for child rearing away from the parents to the government who now felt at liberty to use intervention programmes in order to influence the way very young children are raised. In the United Kingdom the view taken by the government is that 'nothing should be done to remove from parents the responsibility for their children, but that it is in the national interest to help parents discharge their responsibility properly' (DCSF, DWP and HMT 2008, p. 7).

Two of the more well-known US research programmes are the Head Start/Early Head Start and the High/Scope (Perry Preschool Intervention) Programmes.

The Head Start/Early Head Start Programme

Head Start has been running since 1965 and is funded by the Federal government. It is targeted at low-income pre-school children from the age of 4 years, whereas Early Head Start began in 1995 and is aimed at children aged 0–3 years (Gray and Francis 2007). The original Head Start had the aim of helping children to be ready to start school on an equal footing with their peers. Early Head Start was devised as a consequence of a growing body of research that highlighted the importance of the period spanning 0–3 years for later development. The project targets low-income families with at least one child age 0–3 years and aims to enhance children's social, emotional and cognitive development. Parents are given help to improve their parenting and to achieve economic independence (Gray and Francis 2007). The Head Start research evidence has also emphasized the importance of community development if the intervention is to prove successful.

The researchers concluded that Early Head Start could influence cognitive, language, and social–emotional development in very young children from poverty-level families. This happens one or two years before the children typically begin pre-kindergarten programmes. The success of these programmes suggested that 'targeted community based programmes to tackle social exclusion were effective' (Glass 1999, p. 259). However, Harpin and Pennington (2007) also point out that research from the Head Start programme demonstrated that if the programme was expanded without adequate funding, the quality of the input for individual families was compromised. Ormerod (2005) also highlighted the finding that although white families benefited from taking part in the Head Start programme, there was no evidence of significant gains for black families.

The High/Scope Programme

From 1962 to 1967, Weikart et al. in Michigan ran the High/Scope Perry Preschool Programme for young children to help them avoid school failure and related problems. The participants were 58 African American children from low socio-economic status backgrounds and with low IQ scores. Those who began at age 3 received 2 years of services while 4-year-olds received 1 year. The programme provided high quality staffing and learning opportunities, with low pupil–teacher ratios. Participants from the experimental (research) and control (those without extra support) groups have been followed through to age 40.

Amongst the significant benefits attributed to participating in the programmes were that participants were much more likely to finish their education (particularly females in the study, with 84 per cent graduating from high school against 32 per cent in the control group), earn more, avoid drug addiction and raise their own children. There was also an economic benefit to society; every tax dollar invested in early childhood provision saved 17 dollars.

Overall the authors concluded that high-quality pre-school programmes for young children living in poverty contributed to their intellectual and social development in childhood and their school success, economic performance and reduced commission of crime in adulthood. This study suggests that the long-term effects are lifetime effects (Nores et al. 2005).

The research from these American early intervention programmes was important because it demonstrated that pre-school intervention did not just have educational benefits but health and social benefits too which included a considerable cost benefit – investing in early intervention could be economically advantageous to society. It also put a greater emphasis on families, parental involvement and required different agencies to work together collaboratively (Ball 1994 cited in Weinberger et al. 2005). However, it has taken many years for this evidence to become available: the children involved had to grow up before it could be established whether or not taking part in the early intervention programme had been beneficial.

Reflection

Consider these intervention programmes and list which parties gain from taking part in such a programme and in what ways they benefit.

- How does this fit with the earlier beliefs that parents should be responsible for their children?
- Who do you think should be responsible for raising children?

The New Labour policy agenda

New Labour were elected into government in 1997 and had promised in their election manifesto to combat child poverty and increase social inclusion, revitalize the labour market and increase standards in education. Promises linked to childcare policy included trying to move people from 'welfare to work'. One of the ways the government has sought to achieve this is through the New Deal for lone parents through which government is committed to providing accessible and affordable childcare (Penn and Randall 2005). The government also implemented the Sure Start programme whose central aim was to help to eradicate child poverty by 2020. Finally the government also recognized that many women have no choice but to go out to work. Between 1990 and 2000 the UK day nursery market quadrupled (Ball and Vincent 2005).

The government then took steps to alter the nature of, and the way services for young children and their families were delivered (Sylva and Pugh 2005). The National Childcare Strategy (DfEE 1998) led to changes that extended beyond the provision of education. It proposed the setting up of 25 Early Excellence Centres which would serve as models of high quality educare provision and the development of a neighbourhood nursery programme which was intended to bring affordable care to disadvantaged areas. OfSTED inspection of part time nursery education places for all 4-year-olds was also proposed.

The Green Paper *Meeting the Childcare Challenge* was published in 1998 and extended free part-time nursery education to 3-year-olds. The responsibility for overseeing the provision transferred from the Department of Health to the Department of Education and Employment(DfEE). The DfEE was expected to now take the lead in setting up 'joined up' integrated provision and services for young children and their families (Sylva and Pugh 2005).

In addition to this, the New Labour Government instituted a Comprehensive Spending Review (CSR) to review how money was currently being spent and, in turn, how it could now be spent in order to address the above priorities of the new government. Early years policy was the responsibility of several departments and so a series of cross-cutting reviews were undertaken, 'of which the most significant were . . . the review of services for young children' (Glass 1999, p. 259).

Although the original remit of the Treasury-led Review was to look at children who were under 8, it was soon realized that the problems in delivering effective provision were focused on the early years. In addition there was the previously discussed evidence that successful intervention in the earliest years could potentially make a significant difference in terms of positive outcomes for children (Glass 1999).

Early on in the Review agencies other than the usual government departments became involved (Baldock et al. 2005) such as the National Children's Bureau (NCB), early years services, influential academic figures and the Pre-School Learning Alliance (PLA). This involvement of people outside of central government in designing policy was a distinctive feature of the development of the Sure Start programme, as was the attempt to base the development of the policy on research evidence (Glass 1999). Whether research findings gathered in the United States can confidently be applied to UK society appears to be a point that was not debated. According to Norman Glass (2005), who chaired the Treasury working group that proposed the original Sure Start, the resulting policy was child centred, which at that time was highly unusual. However although Sure Start was undoubtedly more child orientated than previous policies, it would be difficult for a policy for which there was such a strong economic imperative to be truly 'child centred'.

The launch of Sure Start

The original Sure Start programme was announced in July 1998 by Gordon Brown, who was then the Chancellor of the Exchequer. Each Sure Start Local Programme (SSLP) was intended to be a community-based programme that could be adapted in order to meet the specific needs of the community it served. The individual SSLPs could provide the services in whatever way they wished provided that they adhered to the key objectives and provided five core services:

1. Outreach and home visiting
2. Support for families and parents

3. Good quality play, learning and childcare
4. Primary and community health care and advice about child and family health
5. Support for children and parents with special needs. (Melhuish et al. 2007, p. 544)

The proposal was that there would be about 250 programmes that would be based in areas of deprivation but would be open to everyone in the area, not just poor families.

> They were to bring together, in a 'joined-up' way, core programmes of health (child and maternal), early education and play, and family support for the under-fours. There was to be an emphasis on outreach to access difficult-to-reach families, and autonomy for local projects to add extra services of their choice, such as debt counselling, benefits advice and so on. (Glass 2005)

The emphasis was to be on parental involvement and using local expertise so that the concerns of the local community could be addressed (Oliver et al. 1998).

This has been described as a 'bottom-up' approach whereby importance was placed on parental involvement and autonomy was given to the SSLPs in order to try and narrow the gap between deprived and non-deprived neighbourhoods as a way of tacking social exclusion and improving services (Melhuish et al. 2007). However, this implies that the bottom of the policy chain is located in families and the community rather than the children. A policy based in the contextual reality of children's lives is helpful for children but it does not make it the 'child centred' approach that Glass (1999) claimed it to be. Although the SSLPs were given the objectives of improving children's social/emotional development as well as their health and learning, there is no evidence that the children were consulted; as is often the case, the children were invisible in the development of this policy that was designed to have a major impact on their lives.

The first SSLPs were established in 1999 and the enthusiastic reception that the programme received led the government to expand the programme to 550 projects in July 2000. This decision was taken *without the government having received any evidence to suggest that the approach was working.* Rutter (2006) suggests that this unusual move was a political one: 'the government had trumpeted the expectation that Sure Start *would* drastically reduce child poverty and social exclusion – the implication being that they "knew" that it would be effective' (p. 136).

Although there were similarities between the designs of the SSLPs and the US research programmes, there was a difference in their aims: whereas the US programmes were intended to prepare children for school, the Sure Start programme was designed to address poverty and social inclusion, although it could be reasonably expected that the children would be better prepared for schooling as a consequence of the intervention.

Reflection

- Do you think that the emphasis on family and community input was pragmatic and potentially effective or do you think the lack of input from children was problematic?

- Do you think that consulting children about the priorities of the SSLPs would have improved the provision for children, or indeed for families and the community?

- How might you usefully consult young children?

What is the wider policy context surrounding the Sure Start agenda?

The national context

Following the 2001 election the Labour government quickened its reform agenda and introduced a number of policies which radically changed Sure Start. This had a significant impact upon the Sure Start programme; some would argue that Sure Start has changed so much that it has effectively been quietly abolished (Glass 2005).

2001–2003

In 2001 central responsibility for and control of early years was transferred from health to education. Early years providers were no longer expected to provide just care; they were also expected to educate the children in their care. This led to the coining of the term 'educare', and the responsibility for quality assuring this provision was transferred to OfSTED in England.

In 2002 *Birth to Three Matters* (DfES 2002) was published with the intention of improving the quality of the provision for this age group. This focus on the needs of young children was welcomed by some (Baldock et al. 2005), whilst others were concerned by the attempt to legislate for the experience of the very youngest children.

In 2003 the Green Paper, *Every Child Matters* (ECM) (DfES 2003a) was published following the report by Lord Laming into the murder of Victoria Climbie and was deployed by government to support their claims that more change was necessary. In the same year came an announcement that was very significant for the Sure Start programme. In November 2002 the inter-departmental Childcare Review proposed the idea of Children's Centres. These would be based on the lessons learned from Sure Start and would be providers of integrated care and education, family support, health services and child-minder support. The Children's Centres would be

> one-stop central hubs for children under five and their families. Centres serving the most deprived areas have access to family healthcare, advice and support for parents including drop-in sessions, outreach services, integrated early education and childcare and links through to training and employment . . . Children's centres help parents find and use a range of employment related services. By working with centres, Jobcentre Plus can overcome problems about accessibility and trust among customers who might otherwise be excluded and better support parents and carers, particularly from the most disadvantaged families, who wish to consider training and employment (DCSF, DWP and HMT 2008, p. 48)

In 2003 the government announced that they were going to establish a Children's Centre in every local authority ward. Although the most deprived 20 per cent of wards would get their centres first, the significance of this announcement was that the provision through Sure Start would eventually be distributed across *all* wards rather than being specifically targeted at areas in need.

Excellence and Enjoyment: National Primary Strategy (DfES, 2003) which was published in 2003 developed the theme of integrated working beyond the early years and into the primary school years. It outlined plans for schools to develop partnerships with parents and the local community as well as propos-ing that schools should develop into extended schools. The extended schools were to work with local providers, agencies, and in many cases other schools to provide access to the core offer of extended services in order to provide 'wrap around care'. In the case of primary schools there were a varied range of activities including study support activities. Childcare was to be provided from 8 a.m. to 6 p.m. for 48 weeks of the year for primary schools. Secondary schools were to provide a safe place to be from 8 a.m. to 6 p.m., parenting and family support was to be provided along with swift and easy access to specialist services such as speech therapy and community use of facilities including adult and family learning and ICT (DCSF, DWP and HMT 2008).

Reflection

- Look at what the government says the role of the Children's Centre is. How are parents positioned in this and how are children positioned?
- Do you think that the economic agenda of getting parents back to work is primarily aimed at helping the children or the economy at large?
- Now look at the provision being offered by the extended schools. How are children and parents positioned here?

The Children's Centres came under the Sure Start programme, as did the Neighbourhood Nurseries Initiative and Early Excellence Centres so that the Sure Start programme was now an umbrella term for a variety of early years provision. Glass (2005) has criticized this move, arguing that Sure Start has been captured by the 'employability agenda' and effectively been abolished. His argument is that in the process there has been a shift from Sure Start being child centred to becoming a childcare agenda to support maternal employment. Pugh and Duffy (2006) state that the Children's Centres are much less generously funded and Glass (2005) points out that they are losing the autonomy in comparison to the original Sure Start projects. Gray and Francis (2007) cite Cohen et al. (2004) who pointed out that as long as the Treasury plays a leading role in the field of early childhood policy, it is not surprising to find that the parental employment agenda is marginalizing other objectives.

It is also worth reminding ourselves of the finding from the Head Start programme mentioned on p. 12 that if the programme was expanded without adequate funding, the quality of the input for individual families was compromised (Harpin and Pennington 2007). The less generous funding combined with the rapid expansion of the Children's Centres may mean that the government is creating conditions that are likely to decrease the effectiveness of any intervention made.

2004–2008

It was announced that there would be 2500 Children's Centres open by 2008 and 3500 by 2010 (DfES 2004b). What has to be recognized is that availability as well as affordability of child care is important here. The Daycare Trust

(2005) estimate that if there are 3500 Children's Centres there will potentially be 800 children trying to access the average of 50 places provided by each centre. A fact that has proven to be very important in evaluating the success of the Sure Start programme is that half of all children that live in poverty do not live in deprived areas (Daycare Trust 2005). This should make the expansion of the programmes across all areas a positive move, however funding will only stretch so far. Children's Centre's in less deprived areas are likely to be offering a far more limited provision and so it could be argued that half of the target population are therefore being denied access to the full range of provision.

By 2005 SSLPs were functioning as Children's Centres and by 2006 they were placed under the control of the Local Authorities (DfES 2008). Thus it could be argued that Glass (2005) is correct in his assertion that Sure Start itself no longer exists. The community driven SSLPs have now been replaced by the less well resourced Children's Centres which may not have the same degree of flexibility in their provision to address the specific needs of the communities in which they are based. The reality is that there are to be more Children's Centres than SSLPs and it is not possible to fund the increased number of centres at the same level as the SSLPs. Government has therefore decided to expand the provision by decreasing the amount of funding that it gives to each Centre, ignoring research evidence that this might lead to a decrease in the effectiveness of the programme (Harpin and Pennington 2007).

Reflection

- Assuming that financial limitations mean that it is not possible to fund all of the services that children might need, do you think that it is acceptable to target the more deprived areas, even if it means neglecting those vulnerable children who are not living in a deprived area?
- Do you think this is a child-centred decision or an economic one?

The year 2004 also saw government reaction to those critics of its original early years policy who claimed it was focused on an economic agenda in that it was trying to get people into work and off welfare, thus placing the needs of children second. Government disputed this, claiming that the aim of their changes was to reduce child poverty and thus centralize children but the critics were not convinced. The government tried to address these concerns with the launch of the ten-year childcare strategy (DfES 2004a) which emphasized the benefits of pre-school education for children. It could be argued that its aim of creating a childcare market 'in which every parent can access affordable, good quality childcare' (p. 1) was still pursuing the 'off welfare into work' economic agenda.

Like Sure Start, the ten-year childcare strategy (DfES 2004a) was based on research evidence, most of which was based on findings from a longitudinal research project 'the Effective Provision of Pre-school Education' (EPPE) project (Sylva et al. 2004).

Reflection

The Effective Provision of Pre-School Education (EPPE) project

This is the first major European longitudinal study of a national sample of young children's development between the ages of 3 and 7 years. The EPPE team collected a wide range of information on 3,000 children who attended 141 settings covering a wide range of providers such as nurseries, playgroups and integrated centres. Their results were compared with a sample of 'home' children (who had no or minimal pre-school experience) who were recruited to the study at entry to school. Twelve settings in which the children had positive outcomes were also studied intensively.

Key findings

Impact of attending a pre-school centre

- Pre-school experience, compared to none, enhances children's development.
- The duration of attendance is important with an earlier start being related to better intellectual development and improved independence, concentration and sociability.
- Full time attendance led to no better gains for children than part-time provision.
- Disadvantaged children in particular can benefit significantly from good quality pre-school experiences, especially if they attend centres that cater for a mixture of children from different social backgrounds.

The quality and practices in pre-school centres

- The quality of pre-school centres is directly related to the intellectual/cognitive and social/behavioural development of children.
- Good quality can be found across all types of early years settings although overall quality was higher in integrated settings, nursery schools and nursery classes.

o Settings which have staff with higher qualifications, especially with a good proportion of trained teachers on the staff, show higher quality and their children make more progress.
o Where settings view educational and social development as complementary and equal in importance, children make better all round progress.
o Children tend to make better intellectual progress in fully integrated centres (centres that fully combine education and care) and nursery schools.

The importance of the home environment

The quality of the learning environment of the home (where parents are actively engaged in activities with children) promoted intellectual and social development in all children. What parents do is more important than who they are.

(Sylva et al. 2004)

Reflection

- Reflect upon each of the findings outlined above. What are the implications for:
  o the parents of a pre-school child?
  o the manager of a pre-school provision?
  o the early years practitioner?
  o the child?
- Do you think that getting parents back to work may be beneficial for the early years child?

The publication of *Every Child Matters: Next Steps for Children* (DfES 2004b) and the passing of the Children Act (DfES 2004c) were very influential with regards to children's provision. The former outlined five outcomes that all children should achieve:

1. Be healthy
2. Stay safe
3. Enjoy and achieve
4. Make a positive contribution
5. Achieve economic well-being

The latter gave most of these outcomes legal status and placed a duty on workers to cooperate in order to achieve these outcomes. It also aimed to place children at the heart of the policy agenda by creating the post of a Children's

Commissioner, a Minister for Children and the creation of Children's Trusts in all Local Authorities who had the responsibility for integrating all child and family services at a local level.

In 2005 *The Children's Workforce Strategy: Every Child Matters: change for children outcomes framework* (DfES 2005a) was published. The strategy proposed an increase in the skills of the workforce; a response to Sylva et al.'s (2004) EPPE study findings that the higher quality pre-school settings had better qualified staff working in them. The Children's Workforce Development Council (CWDC) was created to oversee the development of a suitable skills and career development pathway for early years professionals who were not teachers. The led to the development of Early Years Professional Status (EYPS), a graduate-level qualification that has been offered by accredited providers since 2007.

The Childcare Act built on proposals in the ten-year strategy (DfES 2004a) when it placed new legal duties on Local Authorities. These were that they had to improve outcomes for all children under 5, secure sufficient childcare for working parents and improve information for parents. The Act also promoted further provision of childcare via Children's Centres and Extended schools as had been outlined in an earlier policy document (DfES and DWP 2006). Critically, the Act also removed the distinction between early education and childcare for under-5s by establishing a new *statutory* curriculum for pre-school children – the *Early Years Foundation Stage,* to be implemented from 2008 (DfES 2007b). As well as the statutory nature of the curriculum, critics have been concerned about the obstacles the legislation produces for those seeking to offer educational alternatives to those required in the legislation, for example, Montessori or Steiner schools.

Further evidence of the government recognizing the importance of children and their families was the creation of a new department in 2007. The Department for Children, Schools and Families (DCSF) was created in order to assume responsibility for all issues affecting children up to the age of 19. The first major policy document produced by the Department was the *Children's Plan* (DCSF 2007) which aimed 'to make England the best place in the world for children and young people to grow up' (p. 5). The plan was based upon five principles:

- Government does not bring up children – parents do – so government needs to do more to back parents and families.
- All children have the potential to succeed and should go as far as their talents can take them.

one of
the principles

- Children and young people need to enjoy their childhood as well as grow up prepared for adult life.
- Services should be shaped by and be responsive to children, young people and families.
- It is always better to prevent failure than tackle a crisis later (DCSF 2007, pp. 5–6).

Reflection

- Look at the principles of the *Children's Plan* (2007). How central are children in these principles?

The international policy context

In 1989 the United Nations Convention on the Rights of the Child (UNCRC) was ratified. This stated that children have the right to be protected from illness and neglect, receive an education, be protected from abuse and to be listened to. A legal framework to enable this to happen in the United Kingdom was provided primarily by the Children Acts of 1989 and 2004 (Lancaster 2006). Article 5 of the UNCRC states that there should be an increasing transfer of responsibility for decision making from the adult to the child as the child gets older.

The government has tried to fulfil its obligations to the UNCRC through its policies such as ECM (DfES 2004b) and the *Children's Plan* (DCSF 2007). However, a report produced by UNICEF (2007) suggested that the government still has a long way to go. The report was the first study of childhood across the world's industrialized nations which looked at 40 indicators from the years 2000–2003 including poverty, family relationships and health. The resulting 'league table' that was produced put the United Kingdom at the bottom out of 21 countries. The Children's Commissioner for England, Professor Sir Al Aynsley-Green, said: 'We are turning out a generation of young people who are unhappy, unhealthy, engaging in risky behaviour, who have poor relationships with their family and their peers, who have low expectations and don't feel safe.' (UNICEF 2007). It should be pointed out that the data were gathered prior to implementation of ECM and the subsequent policies. Hopefully the United Kingdom will fare better on these measures in future years if the policies have the desired effect.

Reflection

- To what extent do you think the government is fulfilling its obligations with regards to children?
- Whose needs are being addressed and in what way by the current policy aims?

There have been many new major policies introduced by the Labour government which have changed the type and status of early years beyond recognition. Nutbrown et al. (2008) point out that there has been roughly one major policy a year and the intentions outlined in the *Children's Plan* suggest that this rate of policy production is unlikely to slow down in the near future. The UNCRC (1989) has been a major policy driver for the government and within the policies discussed many rights issues are addressed. A further policy driver is created by the requirement for the government to report back to the UN every five years on the progress it has made against the UNCRC objectives.

Does Sure Start give a good start to life?

From the beginning of Sure Start a national evaluation programme based at Birkbeck College, University of London was begun. Its first phase of evaluation finished in 2005. The second evaluation phase was undertaken between spring 2005 and summer 2007. Data from all of the SSLPs that had been set up between 1999 and 2003 were collected and analysed. Data were also collected from families in Sure Start areas who had not been involved with their local programme.

The National Evaluation of Sure Start (NESS)

First phase evaluation

The initial evaluation published in June 2003 focused primarily on justifying the need for SSLPs (DfES 2003b) and established that the SSLP areas were extremely deprived and that there could be little doubt that the young children in these areas were suffering from multiple disadvantages.

The next stage of the evaluation was published in November 2005 (DfES 2005b) and these initial results suggested that the Sure Start programme was not having the effect that the government had hoped for because there was very little evidence that SSLPs achieved their goals of increasing service use. More worryingly the most deprived children appeared to be worse off living in an SSLP area. The authors emphasized that the results must be treated cautiously because the programme had not been running for long enough to draw any firm conclusions.

These results led to calls from within the right-wing press for the programme to be abandoned. Rutter (2006) pointed out that these calls were premature because the findings were inconclusive. However he also had grave concerns with regards to the methodology of the evaluation. Although he recognized that the design being utilized was the best one available, it was, in his opinion, still very problematic. This is because the provisions offered varied tremendously and none of the areas had to specify precisely what they were doing. This huge variation between the different programmes meant that it was impossible to draw any firm conclusions about whether or not the interventions were beneficial to children.

The next evaluation report published in June 2007 (DfES 2007a) contained grounds for cautious optimism. This evaluation looked at data gathered in a five-year period up to 2005. Some of the tentative conclusions drawn were that fewer children were experiencing economic deprivation and that children aged 11+ were improving their academic achievements. A greater number of children with special educational needs were being identified and there was an increase in the amount of full day care provision. However, this latter finding did not apply to areas with more Black and Minority Ethnic (BME) residents.

Although there are some positive findings reported here, the longstanding criticism that the programmes were failing to reach those families that most needed help and members of the BME community was still valid. Interestingly, this links in with the Head Start findings (Ormerod 2005) mentioned earlier which found that Head Start programmes tended to benefit white families rather than black families.

August 2007 brought a further barrage of criticism from the right-wing press with the publication of the results of a six-year study of 35,000 children carried out by Durham University (Times Educational Supplement 2007). They measured the cognitive development of the children on entry into primary school between 2001 and 2006 and concluded that the cognitive abilities of the children had not increased, nor had the gap in achievement narrowed between children from poor families and those from affluent ones (Durham University 2007).

A further difficulty for the government arose during the same week as the Durham University report when they published data on the achievement of England's 7-year-olds in maths, reading and writing. These children included those children who had been the first beneficiaries of the SSLPs. Unfortunately the figures showed no improvement in maths and reading and a decline in writing ability (Henry 2007).

Evaluation second phase

The study published in March 2008 (DfES 2008) gave grounds for cautious optimism. The data collection period for this study was from spring 2005 to summer 2007. Because of the policy changes previously outlined, SSLPs that were studied in this time period were different to previous evaluations in that they were now functioning as Children's Centres under Local Authority control.

Despite the limitations with regards to the firmness of any conclusions drawn, the results of the study were very different to the results found by the first phase of the evaluation (DfES 2005b). In particular, they found that in contrast to the earlier findings, the more deprived families were *not* being adversely affected by being in a SSLP area. The researchers acknowledged that this important change in the findings may be due to methodological differences. However, they thought it was more likely to be due to the fact that the children in the second phase of the evaluation had spent a longer time being exposed to the programmes. The other contributory factor they identified was that the programmes had matured into higher quality provision (DfES 2008). Although the benefits identified could probably be attributed to the SSLPs, the differences were only modest and so the case for the Sure Start programme was by no means proven.

The pressure on the government continued to build. In June 2008 it was announced that the number of children living in poverty had increased by 100,000 for the second year in a row (Booth 2008). The chance of the government hitting its target of halving child poverty by 2010 and eradicating it completely by 2020 became very unlikely. The definition of relative poverty was living in a household with an income of less that 60 per cent of median earnings. The March 2007 figures showed that there were 2.9 million children living in relative poverty in the United Kingdom as compared to 3.4 million in 1999 when Labour made the original pledge. This level of poverty was also highlighted in June 2008 in a dossier presented to the United Nations by the four Children's Commissioners in which they reported widespread infringements of the human rights of children as outlined in the UNCRC (1989).

The Commissioners criticized the government for not targeting the children who are at greatest risk, including BME children, asylum seekers and children leaving care (Carvel 2008).

In 2008 the government announced a series of new initiatives to try to tackle child poverty and increase social mobility. These measures included a new Child Development Grant of around £200 available to low income parents with children under the age of 5 in ten local authorities from early 2009. Only parents who take up services such as their free entitlement childcare places, and who work with children's centre staff to take agreed action to support their child's development and improve their families' well-being would be eligible. Enhanced work focused services, helping parents to enter and progress in work, were promoted through the £7.6 million that was made available to 30 Children's Centres across ten local authorities.

> **Reflection**
>
> - It can be seen that the economic agenda is dominant in these latest proposals. What does this mean for the Government's claims that they are putting children first?
> - Given the levels of deprivation experienced by children in these SSLP areas, do you think it matters whether the intervention is being driven by an economic or child centred agenda, provided that the outcomes show that the child is benefiting?

What do the users of the provision say?

This chapter has concerned itself with the views of the government and other agencies. Before closing it is important to also reflect on some of the views of the people who have had the opportunity to use their Sure Start/Children's Centre. The Growing Strong report by the National Children's Home (NCH) found that their 48 participants tended to support the idea of universal provision of Sure Start Children's Centres and the services they offer. This was particularly true amongst current users of the centre. Bagley and Ackerley (2006) in their case study of an SSLP reported that the parents were empowered by being involved with the SSLP. Henry (2007) reports how some mothers in Leicester split their experience of being parents into 'before Sure Start' and 'after Sure Start' and quotes one mother for whom it has been very helpful:

> 'it's been brilliant . . . If the centre hadn't been here I would have fallen into the trap of just staying at home and talking to my baby. Instead I've been able to come

and see the health visitor; I've been to the talking babies class; book time; breast feeding workshop and baby massage'.

Overall, the centres have been welcomed by their users. The problem is that they are struggling to reach the most deprived families and in some areas such as London, they have been attracting too many middle-class mothers. This is an issue that still has to be fully addressed by the professionals within the centres. It could be argued that removing the autonomy of the centres and losing community input in the process would not solve the problem since hard to reach families are more likely to respond to advances from within their community rather than official figures who they may distrust. The government has now announced that it is going to fund an extra two outreach workers in the most deprived areas in order to try and tackle this issue (DCSF, DWP and HMT 2008).

Conclusion

The Labour government has undoubtedly significantly raised the profile of early years provision since they came to power in 1997. However, a mixed message has been sent out by government to parents: on the one hand the quality of the relationship they have with their children plays a very important role in determining their outcomes. On the other hand parents need to go to work in order to earn their way out of poverty. It can be argued that the provision of wrap around care and the targets the government has set itself suggest that it is the 'welfare to work' economic agenda that has continued to dominate the policy agenda. This is perhaps not surprising given the central role of the Treasury in the formation of early years policy.

The original SSLPs were unique in their design but this format was replaced with the cheaper Children's Centre option. Nevertheless the evaluation of the offering suggested that intervening in the early years might make a difference to the deprived children at whom it was targeted. Other research evidence such as that from Head Start suggests that it will take years for the benefits of such interventions to take effect and the question is whether governments will have the foresight to keep funding the programme for the many years it will take before a significant difference could be seen.

Perhaps the critics of Sure Start in whatever form it takes need to be more realistic in their expectations. Harpin and Pennington (2007) suggest that 'effective early intervention is not really about a "Head Start." It is about practical support to enable disadvantaged children to start their lives as close to the starting line as possible' (p. 654). This does seem realistic; however, it is also worth pointing out that this statement implies that childhood is a race that begins at school entry and that the early years is all about preparing for that race; that it is a time of 'becoming' rather than 'being'. This seems an impoverished view of childhood; however, government and policy makers appear to view the early years period in just these terms- as a time for acquiring the basic skills a child will need in order to ultimately 'make a positive contribution' and 'achieve economic well-being' (DfES 2004a). Thus far, it would appear that Sure Start may be helping children to get closer to the starting line but problems with the design of the intervention mean that we are unlikely to know for quite some time whether we can say this with any confidence. Whose childhood? Certainly not the child's.

Summary

- The success of American early intervention programmes provided some research evidence for Sure Start, a programme aimed at tackling child poverty and social exclusion. The American programmes also demonstrated that state intervention in children's early experiences could be cost-effective in the long term.
- Although Sure Start projects involved significant local involvement in their design, this did not include consultation with children.
- In 2003 Children's Centres began to be established. These were to be set up in *all* areas, not just areas of deprivation. The programme was quickly expanded and the Sure Start projects became Children's Centres, leading to the accusation that Sure Start had effectively been abolished. There was a strong focus on adult employment, particularly maternal employment.
- During the next few years, a number of initiatives continued to emphasize child-care provision, maternal employment, a curriculum from birth, a more skilled early-year's workforce, greater accountability in early year's provision and the aim of an improvement in children's lives.
- There are tensions between these initiatives regarding government involvement in children's early experiences and whether parents are being supported or undercut, and whether children or the economy are the real focus.
- There have been difficulties in evaluating the success of Sure Start. Although there are now some encouraging findings, research on the American programmes would suggest that it will take many years to discover how effective the programme has been.

Recommended Reading

Baldock, P., Fitzgerald, D. and Kay, J. (2009) *Understanding Early Years Policy.* 2nd edn. London: Sage.

This book clearly explains to the reader what policy is and why it is important. It covers the period between 1945 and 2008 and provides an excellent overview of the developments that have led up to the policy developments discussed in this chapter.

Glass, N. (1999) Sure Start: The development of an early intervention programme for young children in the United Kingdom, *Children and Society*, 13, 257–264.

This article provides an excellent discussion of the aims and aspirations of what the original Sure Start programme was intended to be. It provides a useful base against which to compare the provision that is now being offered by the Children's Centres.

DCSF (2007) *The Children's Plan: Building Brighter Futures* [online]. Available at: http://www.dfes.gov.uk/publications/childrensplan/ [Accessed 2 July 2008].

This document outlines the government's intentions over the next ten years for children. It contains many aspirations for improving the lives of children although it lacks the detail as to how all of these aspirations will be met. Nevertheless it provides a comprehensive overview of current policy intentions. A useful summary can also be downloaded from the same address.

Bibliography

Bagley, C and Ackerley, C. L. (2006) 'I am much more than just a mum'. Social capital, empowerment and Sure Start, *Journal of Education Policy*, 21, 6, 717–734.

Baldock, P., Fitzgerald, D. and Kay, J. (2005) *Understanding Early Years Policy*. London: Sage.

Ball, S. J. and Vincent, C. (2005) The 'childcare champion'? New Labour, social justice and the childcare market, *British Educational Research Journal*, 31, 5, 557–570.

Belsky, J., Barnes, J. and Melhuish, E. (2007) *The National Evaluation of Sure Start: Does Area Based Early Intervention Work?* Bristol: Policy Press.

Booth, J. (2008) Child poverty rises for the second year in a row, *The Times* [online]. Available at: www.timesonline.co.uk/news/poliyics/article4102673.ece [Accessed 11 June 2008].

Carvel, J. (2008) Dossier prepared for UN details grim plight of many young people in Britain, *The Guardian* [online] Available at: http://www.guardian.co.uk/society/2008/jun/09/children.youngpeople [Accessed 9 June 2008].

Cohen, B., Moss, P., Petrie, P. and Wallace, J. (2004) *A New Deal for Children? Re-forming Education and Care in England, Scotland and Sweden*. Bristol: Policy Press.

Daycare Trust (2005) *Childcare and Early Years Services in 2004* [online]. Available at: www.daycaretrust.org.uk [Accessed 12 February 2007].

DCSF (2007) *The Children's Plan: Building Brighter Futures* [online]. Available at: http://www.dfes.gov.uk/publications/childrensplan/ [Accessed 2 July 2008].

DCSF, DWP and HMT (2008) *Ending Child Poverty: Everybody's Business* [online]. Available at www.hm-treasury.gov.uk [Accessed 25 June 2008].

DfEE (1998) *Meeting the Childcare Challenge* [online]. Available at: http://www.surestart.gov.uk/publications/?Document=523 [Accessed 21 December 2008].

DfES (2002) *Sure Start: Making a Difference for Children and Families*. Nottingham: DfES.

DfES (2003a) *Birth to Three Matters, an Introduction to the Framework*. London: HMSO.

DfES (2003b) *Characteristics of Sure Start Local Programme Areas: Rounds 1 to 4*. Nottingham: DfES.

DfES (2003c) *Every Child Matters*, Green Paper Cm 5860. London: TSO.

DfES (2003d) *Excellence and Enjoyment: A Strategy for Primary Schools* [online]. Available from: http://www.standards.dfes.gov.uk/primary/publications/literacy/63553/pns_excell_enjoy037703v2.pdf [Accessed 23 March 2008].

DfES (2004a) *Choice for Parents, the Best Start for Children: A Ten Year Childcare Strategy*. London: DfES.

DfES (2004b) *Every Child Matters: Next Steps for Children*. Nottingham: DfES.

DfES(2004c) *The Children Act* [online]. Available at: www.dfes.gov.uk/publications/childrenactreport/ [Accessed 1 June 2008].

DfES (2005a) *Children's Workforce Strategy*, Consultation Paper. London: DfES.

DfES (2005b) *Early Impacts of Sure Start Local Programmes on Children and Families*. Nottingham: DfES.

DfES (2007a) *Changes in the Characteristics of SSLP Areas between 2000/01 and 2004/05*. Nottingham: DfES.

DfES (2007b) *The Early Years Foundation Stage*. Nottingham: DfES.

DfES (2008) *The Impact of Sure Start Local Programmes on Three Year Olds and Their Families*. Nottingham: DfES.

DfES and DWP (2006) *Choice for Parents, the Best Start for children: Making it Happen – An Action Plan for the Ten Year Strategy: Sure Start Children's Centres, Extended Schools and Childcare*. London: DfES.

Durham University (2007) *Government's Early Years Education Measures yet to Make an Impact* [online]. Available at: http://www.dur.ac.uk/news/allnews/?itemno=5685 [Accessed 21 December 2008].

Glass, N. (1999) Sure Start: The development of an early intervention programme for young children in the United Kingdom, *Children and Society*, 13, 257–264.

Glass, N. (2005) Surely some mistake? *The Guardian* [online]. Available at http://education.guardian.co.uk/earlyyears/story/0,15612,1383617,00.html [Accessed 14 February 2006].

Gray, R. and Francis, E. (2007) The implications of US experiences with early childhood interventions for the UK Sure Start Programme, *Child: Care, Health and Development*, 33, 6, 655–663.

Harpin, V. and Pennington, L. (2007) Early intervention: investment in better opportunities for all, *Child: Care, Health and Development*, 33, 6, 653–654.

Henry, J. (2007) The seven year hitch. *The Sunday Telegraph* [online]. Available at www.lexisnexis.com/uk/business/frame.do?tokenKey=rsh-20.728032.97431114… [Accessed 11 September 2007].

Kazimirski, A., Smith, R., Butt, S., Ireland, E. and Lloyd, E. (2008) *Childcare and Early years Survey 2007: Parents' Use Views and Experiences* [online]. Available at: http://www.dfes.gov.uk/research/data/uploadfiles/DCSF-RR025A.pdf [Accessed 28 June 2008].

Lancaster, Y. P. (2006) Listening to young children: Respecting the voice of the child, in Pugh G. and Duffy, B. (eds) *Contemporary Issues in the Early Years*. London: Sage.

Melhuish, E., Belsky J., Anning, A., Ball, M., Barnes, J., Romanuik, H., Leyland, A. and the NESS research team (2007) Variation in community intervention programmes and consequences for children and families: the example of Sure Start Local Programmes, *Journal of Child Psychology and Psychiatry* 48, 6, 543–551.

NCH (2008) *Growing Strong: Attitudes to Building Resilience in the Early Years* [online]. Available at www.nch.org.uk [Accessed 28 June 2008].

Nores, M., Belfield, C. R., Barnett, W. S. and Schweinhart, L. (2005) Updating the economic impacts of the High/Scope Perry Preschool Programme, *Educational Evaluation and Policy Analysis*, 27, 3, 245–261.

Nutbrown, C., Clough, P. and Selbie, P. (2008) *Early Childhood Education*. London: Sage.

Oliver, C., Smith, M. and Barker, S. (1998) *Effectiveness of Early Interventions: Cross-departmental Review of Provision for Young Children*. London: H. M. Treasury.

Ormerod, P. (2005) *The Impact of Sure Start*. London: The Poltical Quarterly Publishing Co. Ltd.

Penn, H. and Randall, V. (2005) Childcare policy and local partnerships under Labour, *Journal of Social Policy*, 34, 1, 79–97.

Pugh, G. (2006) The policy agenda for early childhood services, in Pugh G. and Duffy B. (eds) *Contemporary Issues in the Early Years*. London: Sage.

Pugh, G. and Duffy, B. (eds) (2006) *Contemporary Issues in the Early Years*. London: Sage.

Rutter, M. (2006) Is Sure Start an effective prevention intervention? *Child and Adolescent Health*, 11, 3, 135–141.

Sylva, K., Melhuish, E., Sammons, P., Siraj-Blatchford, I. and Taggart, B. (2004) The Effective Provision of Pre-School Education (EPPE) Project: Findings from Pre-School to the end of Key Stage 1. Nottingham: DfES ref SSU/SF/2004/01.

Sylva, K. and Pugh, G. (2005) Transforming the early years in England, *Oxford Review of Education*, 31, 1, 11–27.

Times Educational Supplement (2007) No pay no gain for under 5's, *Times Educational Supplement* [online]. Available at: www.lexisnexis.com/uk/business/frame.do?tokenKey=rsh-20.495940.69656466… [Accessed 11 September 2007].

UK CRC Children's Commissioners' report to the UN Committee on the Rights of the Child (2008) [online] Available at: http://www.11million.org.uk/resource/31f7xsa2gjgfc3l9t808qfsi.pdf [Accessed 24 June 2008].

UN CRC (1989) United Nations Convention on the Rights of the Child [online]. Available at: http://www.unicef.org/crc/ [Accessed 2 July 2008].

UNICEF (2007) An overview of child well being in rich countries [online.] Available at www.unicef-irc.org/publications/pdf/rc7_eng.pdf [Accessed 12 February 2008].

Ward, H. and Marley, D. (2007) Steady as you go for the under-5s. *Times Educational Supplement* [online] Available at: http://www.lexisnexis.com/uk/business/frame.do?tokenKey=rsh-20.981095. 19036317... [Accessed 11 September 2007].

Weinberger, J., Pickstone, C. and Hannon, P. (2005) *Learning from Sure Start*. Maidenhead: Open University Press.

'How Well Am I Doing On My Outcomes?'

2

Helen Butcher and Jane Andrews

Chapter Outline

'I've got to go in and do my writing now . . .', 4-year-old busy painting with three friends outside called inside to practise letter shapes. Overheard outside a reception class, September 2007

Why focus on outcomes?

The consequences of childhood have been an abiding concern of humankind. Whether as philosophers, theologians, social reformers, psychologists, neurologists, educators, politicians or parents it is the very plasticity of the human infant, in particular her/his mind which has caused thinkers, practitioners and policy makers to attempt to identify factors in early life which have predictable long-term effects.

In this chapter we want to challenge the description *outcomes* as applied to young children's development. It is still common to view childhood, in particular early childhood, as a time of unfettered freedom or the period of our lives when we are least subject to externally generated measurement. However increasing control and regulation of young children's lives by central government (Hallet and Prout 2003; Anning 2006) has resulted in sets of outcomes being used to channel and measure young children's experiences. We are witnessing a shift of emphasis from family to nation (Williams 1989) as government attempts to control more and more inputs to childhood through regulating childcare, the childcare workforce, curriculum and social interventions for children. The twenty-first century in the United Kingdom has, so far, been marked by policy makers' willingness to describe and direct children's potential towards specified outcomes.

Our intention in asking this question from a child's point of view is to assert that children are not simply raw material to be processed for adult purposes. The question confronts us with children's awareness of their social position. It hints at anxiety, literally, 'Do I measure up?', 'Am I good enough?' It suggests an element of performance and self consciousness in young children's responses to expectations placed on them.

We suggest that the description 'outcomes' when applied to children's education and social experiences reflects a coarsening of our imaginings of childhood. A focus on outcomes likens childhood to a linear production model rather than a complex, subtle and varied process. Equally significantly a concern with outcomes embodies the idea that children are in a state of becoming rather than being. In such an environment children and their childhoods are social investments, and adults, whether practitioners, parents or policy makers are supervisors, assessors and administrators of that process. If children's lives are dominated by the need to achieve curricula and social outcomes the question 'Whose Childhood is it?' becomes especially important and we need to ask ourselves the following:

Key Questions

1. What outcomes are we are referring to?
2. How do these outcomes impact on families?
3. What is the effect on childhood of an outcomes agenda?

Before examining these questions we need to pause and reflect on what we understand by children and their childhoods. Where children were once thought to be passive recipients of information about their world (empty vessels), in the past 30 years a combination of brain research, anthropology and sociology has revised our understanding (Sameroff 1987; Gopnik et al. 1999; Montgomery et al. 2003). The idea that children are 'incomplete' and 'incompetent' has been replaced by an understanding that they are active constructors of their worlds; they are 'social actors'. Children are not merely 'becomings', that is, adults in the making, but 'beings' entitled to human rights which include being consulted on issues which concern them. In constructing their unique understandings of the world children act upon and change it. This has led to the study of child development moving away from studying children separately from their social environments to an understanding that studying them in context is vital (Bronfenbrenner 1970; Dunn 1995; Rogoff 2001).

What outcomes are we referring to?

From the considerable volume of social and educational policies relating to children produced since 1997 we want to contextualize and consider three which have explicit outcomes for children and will have a direct impact on reshaping early childhoods into what Hallet and Prout (2003) call 'civic childhood'. They are:

- Every Child Matters (2004)
- EYFS (2007)
- Children's Plan (2007).

Before reviewing each of these overlapping documents it is useful to consider some of the key social, economic and political factors which informed their development. We will simplify a complex picture, which includes gender politics and the changing shape of families, into four features:

1. The price of poverty
2. The labour market
3. Brain research
4. Anxiety about childhood.

The price of poverty

By the mid-1990s the United Kingdom had the highest rate of relative poverty in the EU (HM Treasury, 2001, p. 2). The consequences of lives lived in poverty are hugely expensive not only in restricted life chances but economically, through welfare benefits, lost tax revenue and crime. We know that if a child is born into poverty they have a greater than average chance of dying in similar circumstances. Both as children and adults their health, mental and physical, educational opportunities and economic well being are all significantly affected by a childhood lived in poverty. All this costs governments money. Consequently there has been an increasing focus on the economic effects of early childhood experiences and so in children's potential whether as learners, citizens of a welfare state, future tax payers or potential offenders.

The labour market

There has been a significant shift in social attitudes towards women with young children working outside the home. In the 1950s John Bowlby's (1953) ideas regarding the importance of a child's continuous relationship with her/his mother or mother substitute influenced many families. He developed a concept of 'maternal deprivation' to describe the experience of children who did not experience maternal continuity and associated this separation of infant and mother with delinquency and mental instability. Not surprisingly many families in the 1950s, 1960s and 1970s, provided they could afford it, decided mothers should stay at home. With the assertion of feminist ideas along with research suggesting that care for young children outside the home did not lead directly to delinquency (Tizard 1991) came an expanding labour market. Increasing numbers of women chose to work full or part time outside the home. This created a demand for affordable childcare.

> . . . [A] growing number of mothers working has created a pressing need for childcare. Policy makers, business leaders and parents increasingly recognise the dual role of quality early childhood services in promoting children's cognitive skills, school readiness and social behaviour and in supporting working parents. (Neuman 2005, p.130)

When introducing the Childcare Bill in 2006 Ruth Kelly, then Secretary of State for Education and Skills stated that parents now had a right to expect that high quality childcare should be available for those who require it. In the course of 50 years assumptions regarding responsibility for the provision of childcare had moved from the family to the nation.

Brain research

Gerhardt (2004) reports on the impact neuroscience is making on our understanding of the relationship between social interactions during babyhood and later cognitive and emotional development. The shaping of our brains, our mental architecture, is established early in life and is predicated on babies' need for emotional safety, positive interactions and strong social bonds. Where this is achieved the foundation for successfully processing abstract cognitive demands is possible. Where it is not achieved children grow into adults who have difficulty managing their emotions and consequently often struggle with school learning and, as they grow up, managing their lives.

> Policy interest in the early years has been spurred by brain research, showing that the first few years of life are critical for a child's early development and learning. (Neuman 2005, p.130)

Neuman also draws on the first report on Early Childhood Education and Care (ECEC) from the Organisation for Economic Co-operation and Development (OECD), *Starting Strong* (2001) to remind us that the 'soaring' of policy on early childhood education and care featured in many minority world countries towards the end of the twentieth and beginning of twenty-first centuries.

Anxiety about childhood

As historians of childhood (Jenks 1996; Hendrick 1997) remind us, societal concern about children and childhood is not confined to our own times. It has though formed a significant part of social debate at the beginning the twenty-first century as the congruence of *The Good Childhood Inquiry* (2006), *The Primary Review* (2006) and *Toxic Childhood* (Palmer 2006) testify. The Children's Society, which commissioned Professor Judith Dunn to chair The Good Childhood Inquiry,

> commented on the climate of fear and confusion surrounding children and young people.

This is sometimes characterized, rather dramatically, as the end or death of childhood (Buckingham 2000).

Every Child Matters

It is in the context of the features listed above that the Labour government sought to expand childcare, tackle poverty and improve life chances for all children through a combination of curricula and social interventions. These included the National Literacy Strategy (1998), The Children's Fund (2000) and Sure Start (2001). Figures published in 1997 which showed United Kingdom at bottom of European league for child poverty led to a commitment, in 1999, to halve rates of child poverty by 2010 and eradicate it by 2020.

Then, an event early in 2000 galvanized an already child-focused agenda into the production of a green paper movingly entitled *Every Child Matters* (ECM) which was to affect every child in the country. The event was the murderous neglect of 8-year-old Victoria Climbie living in North London with her aunt, and the spur to action was the inquiry into her death by Lord Laming (2003). Since 1945 there had been nearly 70 reports into the murders of children by their parents or carers. Many had come to the same conclusion as Laming, that it was a failure of agencies responsible for child welfare to communicate with each other which led to the death of the child in question.

So why did this set of 108 recommendations lead to a comprehensive overhaul of the local authority infrastructure for meeting children's needs when previous recommendations had been more sporadic? It may be better to answer this question by saying that Victoria's death, and Laming's resulting recommendations, provided an opportunity for government to expand its sphere of influence over childhoods. This is demonstrated in the radical assertion that, 'child protection cannot be separated from policies to improve children's lives as a whole' (Every Child Matters 2003, p. 5). In other words, as a response to Victoria's death The Children Act 2004 focuses on protection, provision and expectations for all children, not just those in need or risk of significant harm. On the one hand this statement appears logical and coherent, a holistic entitlement for all, on the other it serves to legitimize government in further structuring and shaping childhood.

In terms of the balance of government and family holding information on children perhaps the most dramatic outcome for children was the creation of a database, ContactPoint in 2007, which all children would be entered on. The intention was to promote integrated working amongst professionals working with children and avoid the lack of information sharing which had led to the death of Victoria Climbie. But there are implications regarding children's rights and the question who do children belong to.

ContactPoint is a key element of the Every Child Matters programme to transform children's services by supporting more effective prevention and early intervention. (Every Child Matters 2007)

Less prominent to the general public than the Laming inquiry but equally important in the development of Every Child Matters was the critical review by the United Nations Committee (UNICEF 2002) into the United Kingdom's implementation of the UNCRC, which is also discussed elsewhere in this book. As well as noting some progress towards fulfilling the Convention's articles and welcoming the creation of the Children and Young People's Unit the Committee commented that previous recommendations had still not been addressed. It welcomed the 1998 Human Rights legislation which applied both to children and adults but noted,

> The Committee is concerned that the provisions of the Convention on the Rights of the Child have not yet been incorporated into domestic policy nor is there any formal process to ensure that new legislation fully complies with the Convention. (p. 3)

The stated objectives of ECM were 'a new approach to the well-being of children and young people' with organizations involved with providing services to children teaming up in new ways, sharing information and working together, to protect children and young people from harm and help them achieve what they want in life. This hugely ambitious agenda placed at its core the achievement of five outcomes for all children 0–19.

- Being healthy
- Staying safe
- Enjoying and achieving
- Making a positive contribution
- Achieving economic well being

> These five outcomes need to be at the heart of everything a school does and reinforced through every aspect of its curriculum – lessons, events, routines, the environment in which children learn and *what they do out of school* [our emphasis]. (QCA 2008)

But these outcomes are not only to be achieved in school but in every context where children experience professional care. This will include extended school provision, health care, holiday clubs. For policy makers this represents joined up thinking and cohesion. It provides a clear five-pronged architecture on which to develop Laming's interprofessional agenda. For Hallet and Prout (2003), it increases the experience of the institutionalized child.

You may think it unduly critical for us to call into question such apparently uncontentious aims. After all, who would not want twenty-first century children to enjoy these benefits? Our concern has two elements, first that children are being constructed in the way the adult world wants them to be or at least wants them to want to be. The second is the expanded role of government in young children's lives when it seeks to determine not only the curriculum but beyond it as well, what Cameron (2007), refers to as 'social governance'.

From desirable to required outcomes; tightening and extending curricula control

The first explicit use of outcomes as both a description of, and ambition for young children's learning was in1996 with the publication of *Desirable Outcomes for Children's Learning on Entering Compulsory Education* (DoCL) (SCAA 1996). The intention was to connect pre-school experiences to National Curriculum provision so that children would be ready to learn. Children's learning experiences were divided into six areas, Personal and Social Development, Language and Literacy, Mathematics, Knowledge and Understanding of the World, Physical Development and Creative Development. Critics of this historic intervention in, and specification of, the education of young children pointed out that not only were the areas heavily academic but the broad statements of expectation positioned nursery experiences as preparatory for the next stage rather than valuable in their own right (National Children's Bureau 1998).

The publication of the Curriculum Guidance for the Foundation Stage (CGFS) in 2000 unified the learning experiences and expectations of young children in nurseries and reception. The six areas of learning were retained but what had been a short document became a lengthy 130-page document which specified in great detail what children and their practitioners would be doing and subdivided children's learning into linear stages of development. The key policy change between DoCL and CGFS was the inclusion of all providers of education and care to young children; playgroups, childminders, private or state nurseries were now obliged to use the curriculum guidance even though children in their care were below statutory school age. This centralized control of young children's learning became formalized when the Education Act 2002 extended the National Curriculum to include the foundation stage and the six areas of learning became statutory. In November 2002 the government further extended its reach into young children's lives by publishing Birth to Three Matters (DfES 2002). This introduced a framework for, 'all those who work with, and care for children aged birth to three, including those children with SEN and/or disability'.

The framework itemized lists of outcomes in each of four features of development: A strong child, a skilful communicator, a competent learner and a healthy child. This notion of outcomes for childhood from *birth* represents an unprecedented and dramatic shift in the role of government in the early experiences of children.

The introduction of the Early Years Foundation Stage (2008) to unify the learning outcomes and requirements of children aged 0–5 replaces the distinct documents of Birth to Three Matters and CGFS and is carefully analysed in Chapter 3.

The Statutory Framework for the Early Years Foundation Stage, EYFS (2007) cements the outcomes of Every Child Matters into a curriculum for children from birth onwards.

> The overarching aim of the EYFS is to help young children achieve the five Every Child Matters outcomes. (p. 7)

We need to convey the complexity of this document and how it seems to be constructing children and practitioners. Examining the EYFS can feel a bit like looking into multiple mirrors. There are four themes, A Unique Child, Positive Relationships, Enabling Environments, Learning and Development, supported by four features each of which are sub-divided into three components further detailed with six supporting descriptions. Additionally there is a separate document which matches the EYFS against the UNCRC. The importance of assessing progress continually is heavily emphasized.

Imagine you are in a busy nursery, and all nurseries *are* busy, and have responsibility for monitoring and recording progress regularly against these multiple statements. It seems likely that the task of assessing to provide evidence that children are progressing, in a linear fashion, against the outcomes will become a barrier between children and their educators. We suggest this ever-increasing level of prescription reveals a lack of trust by policy makers of both children and practitioners. One reason why we say this is because countries with significantly less prescription scored much more highly on the Well Being survey, for example, Holland and Denmark. We would like to reflect that the years since 1995, when there was no specification for young children's learning, have seen an increasing prescription, by government, of outcomes for younger and younger children. As Hallet and Prout (2003) argue, 'modernity's drive to control the future through children often leads to attempts to regulate and standardize what they learn and how they learn it.'

To illustrate the fact that in the United Kingdom at the present time there is a move towards measuring and quantifying children's lives and their experiences in childhood it is useful to look at the statistics information on the Department for Children, Schools and Families website. The following reflection box includes some data from the National Results of the Foundation Stage Profile for 2006/07. The website gives many more details but here are some of the statistics reported:

Reflection

The assessment areas with the highest percentage of children working securely within the Early Learning Goals were:

1. Physical development – 88 per cent
2. Mathematical development – *Numbers as labels for counting* – 87 per cent
3. Personal, social and emotional development – *Dispositions and attitudes* 87 per cent

The assessment areas with the highest percentage of children *working towards* (1–3 points) the Early Learning Goals were:

1. Communication, language and literacy: Writing – 15 per cent
2. Communication, language and literacy: Linking sounds and letters – 14 per cent

- Reflect on what this tells us about this use of assessment with young children.
- To what extent is such a model of assessment appropriate for young children, their carers and families? (DCSF 2007a)

The large majority of young children are clearly *not* achieving the outcomes allocated to them in the Literacy goals in the Foundation Stage. Academics reported on their concerns about the appropriateness of the Early Learning Goals within the area of communication, language and literacy in relation to children's use of punctuation. As a result of this expression of concern changes have been made in 2008 to the Early Learning Goals. This question is taken up in the next chapter.

The Children's Plan

Despite the array of initiatives and policies directed towards improving children's welfare and achievement by the government since 1997 a report issued by the UN in 2007 caused great consternation. It led to another over-arching policy document which would be used to direct and organize childhoods from the seat of government for the forthcoming decade. United Nations Report Card 7, *An Overview of the Wellbeing of Children in Rich Countries* (UNICEF 2007) subdivided wellbeing into six dimensions: Material Wellbeing, Health and Safety, Educational Wellbeing, Family and Peer Relationships, Behaviours and Risks and Subjective Wellbeing. The United Kingdom came at the bottom overall of the list of 21 countries surveyed.

Shortly after publication of Report Card 7 the appointment of new ministers brought about by the change of one Labour Prime Minister, Tony Blair, for another, Gordon Brown, provided the opportunity for the re-titling of some government departments. What had been the Department for Education and Skills (DfES) was divided and renamed the Department for Children, Schools and Families (DCSF) with the intention to, '*put the needs of families, children and young people at the centre of everything we do*' (Ed Balls, Secretary of State for Children, Schools and Families, DCSF 2007c).

This change from an abstract to a concrete noun, from education to children, as well as the addition of families indicates a significant reconceptualization in thinking about provision for our youngest citizens by extending its scope far beyond the confines of schools and early years settings. Internationally, as well as nationally, embarrassed by the wellbeing report the new department immediately began a consultation, called Time to Talk (DCSF 2007b). In December 2007 the *Children's Plan* was published (DCSF 2007c). Reviewing its contents indicates a government's willingness to bear some responsibility for all aspects of children's lives, including their happiness. Although the document states, at regular intervals, that, 'families not governments bring up children', its six strategic objectives are to:

1. secure the health and wellbeing of children and young people;
2. safeguard the young and vulnerable;
3. achieve world-class standards;
4. close the gap in educational achievement for children from disadvantaged backgrounds;
5. ensure young people are participating and achieving their potential to 18 and beyond; and
6. keep children and young people on the path to success.

In order to synthesize the aims of Every Child Matters with the Children's Plan in April 2008 the DCSF published an overview, Every Child Matters Outcomes

Framework (DCSF 2008) which tabulates how these two major policy documents inter-relate. Before inviting you to make your own investigation of this framework we would like to draw your attention to one of the national indicators as an illustration of the adult-focused agenda pressing down on children and their childhoods. If you look at the outcome Enjoy and Achieve, one of the national indicators is:

> Achievement of at least 78 points across the Early Years Foundation Stage with at least 6 in each of the scales in Personal Social and Emotional Development and Communication, Language and Literacy.

We would agree with Lilian Katz (1994) who describes this kind of approach to children's development as top-down, whereas the most successful and happiest examples of engaging children – we would point here to Te Whariki, New Zealand, the Netherlands and Reggio Emilia – adopt a bottom-up approach which involves listening to and responding to children's interests and engagements.

Reflection

Go to the Every Child Matters Outcomes Framework website at
http://www.dcsf.gov.uk/childrensplan/downloads/ECM%20outcomes%20framework.pdf

- Select one of the five outcomes and think of a young child you know. Evaluate how effectively the *inspection evidence* and *judgements, targets and indicators* would support her/him achieving that outcome.

As economic effects and social stability are the business of government, so the increasing interest of government in children's early experiences and their enthusiasm for measurable outcomes for children. Vincent and Ball (2005) observe that New Labour's attention to early childhood has provided an unprecedented focus for government policy on children's lives and well-being at the earliest ages. However, while this attention to has been largely aimed at addressing issues of poverty, equality of opportunity and social justice and provoked valuable debate, it also has brought with it a move towards state intervention in the 'private space' of children's home lives.

How do these outcomes impact on families?

So the ten years since Labour formed a government have marked a dramatic change in policy conceptualizations of childhood its form, function and possibilities. Government policy documents have moved towards greater intervention in and attention to what had historically been considered a 'private' space and time. In the United Kingdom, England in particular, there are now so many calls on childhood it can be hard to quantify the number of agencies with vested interests in this stage of life.

This tendency towards greater government intervention in children's early experiences was perhaps foreseen by Urie Bronfenbrenner as far back as 1970 when he conducted his study into childhood in the then USSR and the United States. His description of children's upbringing in the United States was described as follows:

> Over the years, de facto responsibility for upbringing has shifted away from the family to other settings in the society, some of which do not recognise or accept the task. (Bronfenbrenner 1970, p. 95)

This observation may encourage us to return to the question posed in our chapter title which serves as a reminder of the atmosphere of regulation and accountability in which children are growing up in the current time.

In this section we consider how the outcomes agenda and government attention to children and early childhood impacts on families. If the state is beginning to take on roles traditionally considered to belong to the private or home domain then what implications are there for parents and carers?

Parental roles

We might begin by thinking about what parents want for their children. The study of early childhood in a global context, has demonstrated the diversity of experience which the dynamic relationship between culture and childrearing produces for children and adults (Rogoff 2001; Montgomery et al. 2003). Decisions and judgements made, collectively and individually, by those caring for children whether about feeding, sleeping, learning, socializing or working reflect the specific needs and preoccupations of the time and place, that is, culture, in which they live.

> Studies have shown that in all societies, parents tend to promote those specific forms of activity in their offspring that coincide with the values and behaviours which represent the approved norms of that society. (Rabain Jamin 1989, p. 296)

Despite this diversity, LeVine (1988) reminds us that there are three preoccupations, we might say outcomes, common to all parents:

- Survival
- Economic welfare
- Self actualization

So no matter whether we were to reflect on parenting in the past or present, whether in Western societies or the majority world, it would be possible to identify these three concerns in all contexts. We now return to our focus on outcomes for children in the United Kingdom as set out in the Children Act 2004, which are:

> Stay safe
> Be healthy
> Enjoy and Achieve
> Make a positive contribution
> Achieve economic well being

Even a cursory examination of these outcomes reveals a close match between them and the universal pre-occupations of parents. A heavy policy focus on early childhood education and care requires us to ask ourselves who has responsibility for children's well-being and development?

Where government has taken responsibility for expanding the provision of childcare it can choose to define the direction and 'product' of the provision by setting required outcomes from the childcare providers. This invites us to question how far has the state encroached on what has previously been determined by families.

From education to 'educare'

There are new ways of talking about the attention from government to early childhood which we are exploring in this chapter. For example, rather than distinguishing between what happens in children's lives from birth to five and considering that to be care of children, and what happens from 5 onwards, which has traditionally been conceptualized as the time of formal schooling and education, we can come across terms such as 'educare'. The Children's Plan (DCSF, 2007c) states:

> 'Educare' – integrated education and childcare – which can be used flexibly and further developed by the creation of the Early Years Foundation Stage.
> The EYFS removes the existing legal distinction between care and education to better reflect the distinctive nature of provision in the early years – for young children care and learning happen together and are indivisible. (DCSF 2007c, Annex D, p.167)

With the increase in care outside of family settings has come the increase in concern with monitoring and measuring outcomes of interventions. Guidance on the DCSF Parents' Centre website for those caring for children aged 0–3 focuses mainly on providing information about care outside of the family. Also, Ofsted, which has responsibility for inspecting the work of childminders, who obviously work in their own homes, has produced posters which are to be displayed in childminder's homes relating to matters such as health and safety. Such posters provide a concrete reminder of the reach of the state into home settings. How would we feel to have reminders about health and safety in our homes for example a sign saying 'And now wash your hands' in our own bathrooms?

In their survey of research for the Primary Review on 'parenting, caring and educating', Muschamp et al. (2007), concur with points made above, that is, that family structure and formation in the United Kingdom have changed markedly from the context existing at the time of the Plowden report (1967). This means that if attention is being paid to the so-called outcomes of childhood as a way of measuring the effectiveness of government policy and provision, then a broader awareness of who needs to be influenced is necessary.

Bookstart+ illustrates clearly the fine line that is being followed by organizations advising and guiding parents – on the one hand reassuring parents and carers by affirming that 'you know your child best of all', while on the other hand informing them that they need to refer to a professional if they have any concerns 'if you have any concerns about your child's development speak to your health visitor or speech therapist'. You may wish to read through materials on the Bookstart website (www.bookstart.org.uk) and consider how parents and carers are being conceptualized and what language is used to communicate with them about their role of parenting and care.

Tensions between families' roles and the role of the state in children's lives

The possible tensions created by the move toward an increased policy focus on early childhood were referred to by a member of the New Labour government in 1998:

> So far from being a nanny state we must become an enabling state which ensures that parents and families have the backing they need. (Blunkett 1998 cited in Reynolds 2005, p. 5)

The above quotation indicates an awareness that for the state to appear to be telling parents how to bring their children up would be a step too far and that, in the view of Blunkett at least, a more acceptable approach would be for the state to provide more support for parents. This particular role for government policy is repeated in the Children's Plan (2007c) in the following quotation:

> Parents bring up children, not governments, and we want this Children's Plan to mark the beginning of a new kind of relationship in which the government commits to working in close partnership with families at every level . . . (p. 15)

Reynolds (2005), from the National Family and Parenting Institute, tackles this question of who is responsible for children's care and development when considering government policies in relation to children's learning. He notes that what constitutes parents' and the state's responsibilities regarding the particular issues relating to children's learning can be an area where tensions lie. For example, certain government initiatives may serve to reduce 'parents' direct input into their children's lives' (Reynolds 2005, p. 3). You may wish to read more about the work of the NFPI on their website at www.nfpi.org and explore their perspective on parenting and the role of the state further.

A parallel concern about roles and responsibilities, this time between schools and parents, has been expressed. Fears about the effects of the reach of schools into children's home lives have been voiced: Edwards and Warin (1999) asked whether homes are being 'colonised' by schools and Marsh (2003) has referred to a flow of 'one-way traffic' from nurseries to homes.

In addition, the following reflections from the Primary Review warn of the risks of the diversity of children's home lives, in terms of cultural practices, being stifled if an overly controlling approach to policy and practice is taken. You may wish to reflect on the language used to express these ideas and we have added **bold** to emphasize terms we found thought-provoking.

> [A]s children's lives become increasingly '**scholarised**' they may wish to defend the home as their private space. Children and parents may also resist current moves to increase 'parental involvement' by turning the home into an **educational environment**. Parents will have to consider how far to protect their children against **scholarisation** and how far they help them engage with it. Free time for young children is an important issue here. So too is the need for the education service to accept that many children contribute to the family division of labour and that school work is not the only **educationally productive activity** in which they engage. (Mayall 2007, p. 14)

The Children's Plan clearly indicates that the government is conscious of the potential tension present in its policies by stressing the continued importance of families and parents and stating that it was not seeking to replace them.

Parents and families matter?

As well as the political expediency of avoiding offending a large number of voters by implying that they do not know how to bring up their children, interest has been growing in recent years in the important roles that parents might play in their children's *learning* lives. In 2000 the Institute for Public Policy Research published a report entitled 'Parents matter OK!?', a title which is quoted from a graffiti slogan seen on a school wall in Hackney, London in 1998. The report provides consideration of ways in which schools and parents might work more closely together for the benefit of children's learning. One of the points raised in the report is that parents' influence might be most effective, not in participating in the life of the school (helping in class or fundraising, for example), but through providing support for their children at home.

The role of adults in children's lives at school age tends to be discussed in terms of understandings held by teachers and parents or carers about children's lives in and out of school. Researchers have made calls for what they conceptualize as these 'two worlds' or simultaneous worlds to be brought closer together or for improved mutual understanding to be achieved (Hughes 2000). The UK government's interest in parents' and carers' roles in their children's learning is evidenced by the attention they get in terms of information – the parents' centre on the DCSF website (www.dfes.gov.uk/parentscentre). The website offers a parent-directed view of schooling. The focus on parents is also evidenced by the fact that the ECM agenda was followed by a document entitled 'Every Parent Matters'. The EPM report focused on balancing a commitment to supporting parents and carers who are identified as needing help with encouraging parents and carers who are deemed to be operating effectively:

> Being a parent is – and should be – an intensely personal experience and parents can be effective in very different ways. However we also have a growing understanding, evidenced from research, about the characteristics of effective parenting. (DCSF 2007d)

The state intervention into family life can be seen to permeate communication with parents about how their role might be played in the business of childrearing.

To return to our original question in this section we asked what role there remains for families in a society where state guidance reaches further into family life. An essential dilemma resides in the government's beliefs that, on the one hand, the government expresses the view that families bring up children while, on the other hand, passing legislation and producing guidance which seeks to guide and regulate children's lives. We might ask ourselves what the cost of such changes in the relationship between the individual and the state might be. What might be lost in terms of diversity in its differing forms (linguistic, cultural, regional) in an effort from the state to share what it defines as the evidence for effective parenting?

What is the effect on childhood of an outcomes agenda?

> Children have preferences which may differ systematically from those of adults, and, furthermore, children's standpoint should be recognized by scholars and activists and incorporated into policy targeted at children and their families.
>
> (Levison 2000, p.125)

So far we have illustrated ways in which the long arm of government now reaches into the lives of young children from birth onwards, and holds on, tightly, with formalized expectations of children and their professional carers whether curricula or social. The financial cost of this high degree of intervention is justified in terms of projected long term social benefits gained from larger numbers of children achieving educational success and a projected reduction in crime, drug abuse and welfare dependency. The intended benefits are proudly trumpeted but what are the unquantifiable costs to children? We have already commented on the creation of a national database for all children but curricula and social outcomes place explicit demands on even very young children by defining and measuring these expectations.

> In an audit culture this imperative to consult has been matched by increasing demands on the potential of children. (Hallet and Prout 2003, p. 11)

In assessing whose childhood it is we should emphasize that it is *adults*: politicians, academics, policy makers and policy implementers, who have formulated and enacted *their* desired outcomes for children. Ironically this intense organization of childhood has occurred alongside increasing pressure, national and international, to listen to children and involve them in decisions concerning their own lives. Despite unquestioningly focusing on children's welfare the three major policies identified above have demonstrated very limited levels of consultation with children, the very 'service users' ECM, EYFS and the Children's Plan are designed for.

> Children's voice should, we believe, be heard much more strongly in the process of policy formation at all levels. (Hallet and Prout 2003, p. 1)

Consulting with children

We have chosen to finish our chapter by asking questions about the impact of an outcomes agenda on childhood. Children's perspectives (Clark et al. 2003; Hallet and Prout 2003) are represented in this part of the chapter, not as an afterthought but rather as a way of leaving you thinking about children, their rights and their voices. As Clark et al. (2003) remind us, the practice of consulting with young children is a minority activity. Certainly the practice makes demands on those working with children. In their work listening to young children's experiences and ideas about fostering and adoption Clark and Statham (2005, p. 45) refer to these demands as 'uncertainty about how to listen to young children'. They also use in their title a very powerful phrase, '*children; experts in their own lives*', which offers valuable provocation to 'expert' adults. Sceptics sometimes ask how reliable are their views, how much do they understand, how much responsibility is it appropriate for them to shoulder? Interestingly these ethical and methodological questions apply equally to consulting with adults. Below is an example of consulting children of ages 3 and 4 regarding the design of their new nursery. But first in order to focus your engagement with this section we would like *you* to collect some children's perspectives.

Activity

Guidance

Ensure you have appropriate permissions before undertaking these activities including permission from children you consult.

Talk with some children, under 8, neighbours, relatives or children you work with, about childhood and adulthood. It can be less intimidating for children if you arrange to talk to a small group of three or four. Try to find a time when you and the children are relaxed and ask some of these questions gently and quietly perhaps when walking along or tidying up. Some young children are more familiar with the word 'grown-up' than adult; you need to find out which is more appropriate for the children you are talking with.

1. Allow them uninterrupted thinking time.
2. Avoid debating with them.
3. Record their answers and note their age.
4. If it feels comfortable a useful follow up to any of their answers can be, 'that's interesting, how do you know?'

Some suggested questions

How old do you have to be to be an adult?
Is it better to be a child or an adult?
What do adults want from children/want children to be like?
What do adults want for children?
What do children want from adults/want adults to be like?
What do you and children you know like and dislike about being a child?

Article 12 of the UNCRC is the most relevant for a consideration of the participation of children.

> States Parties shall assure to the child who is capable of forming his or her own views the right to express those views freely in all matters affecting the child being given due weight in accordance with the age of the child. (Child Rights Information Network website)

Clark et al. distinguish between two forms of consultation: day to day and one off consultation. The example described, very briefly, below is a one-off consultation.

Case Study

In 2006 the University of West of England (UWE) decided to expand nursery provision for students and add a new purpose-built nursery to the main campus. There was popular nursery provision on a smaller campus. Maintaining its positive ethos in the new setting was an important objective. The Project Team was aware of the importance of including children's perspectives in shaping their environment and delegated a subgroup including the project architect to consult children in the existing nursery about the design of the new one.

Before embarking on the consultation the group needed to establish some principles. These were:

1. to be as clear as possible with children;
2. to find ways of giving control to children;
3. to ensure nothing was promised that couldn't be delivered.

The consultation had three parts. Initially children were informed that we wanted some ideas from them about what they liked about their present nursery. To capture this data the children were provided with digital cameras and asked to photograph their favourite parts of the nursery. Immediately after taking the pictures they were loaded onto the nursery computer and children viewed them, commenting and laughing. A member of the adult group identified themes – inside, outside, places for toys, places for artefacts children had made. Once grouped into these themes the images were enlarged, printed on posters and returned to the nursery for discussion with nursery staff.

> The final part of the discussion was an activity afternoon which nursery staff supported by a range of activities – construction, catalogue cutting, drawing – focused on *how my nursery could be even better*. All four members of the group explained who they were and talked with and noted children's ideas as they participated in these activities. In discussion with the architect Shanna (4) said that a nursery would be better with no corners – she illustrated her point by pointing to an area of the nursery with lots of doors in a small space making it very restricted. The architect, mindful of Principle 3 said, genuinely, that he thought her idea was perhaps the best he had heard but because the university had to buy ready made it wouldn't be possible to have a round one but it would be possible to have some round shaped spaces inside. This seemed to satisfy Shanna who went on to insist that there should be beds in the 3/4-year-olds' room. This was incorporated into the interior design. One of the most photographed images was the outside play house which had windows suggesting it had two storeys but it didn't. In discussion with the children several indicated they would prefer a play house that did have two storeys. This also became incorporated into the design. The majority of the children's talk referred to the outside environment which was clearly very important to them. This was prioritized in the new development and at the children's specification included a slope or 'hill' for a wide variety of imaginative and physical play opportunities.

The development of children's rights

In 1998 England created the post of Minister for Children and all four countries in the United Kingdom appointed Children's Commissioners in the 1990s. However progress towards consulting children about matters which affect their lives, which we would argue constitutes appropriate respect for children (Butcher and Lee 2008), has occurred locally, nationally and internationally, but despite commitments in Every Child Matters, EYFS and the Children's Plan we contend that it remains, patchy, ad hoc and often tokenistic (Hart 1997).

It is common to identify the coinciding of two historic events in 1989 as the beginning of a commitment to children's rights. 1989 was the United Nations Year of the Child; it culminated in the adoption by the UN General Assembly of the Convention on the Rights of the Child (UNCRC). In the same year in the United Kingdom The Children Bill was notable for asserting, for the first time, children's right to be consulted, in this case about their preferred living arrangements if their parents separated. In fact a more accurate date for the emergence of the idea of children as rights bearing citizens, albeit with limited rights, is exactly 100 years earlier in 1889 with the passing of the first Act of Parliament which made it illegal to treat a child badly. It was known as the Children's Charter and was largely due to the efforts of Benjamin Waugh who had formed the London Society for the Prevention of Cruelty to Children in 1864. It was renamed the National Society for the Prevention of Cruelty to Children (NSPCC) in 1889. It is worth noting that the creation of a charity dedicated to protecting children from cruelty came exactly 60 years after the creation of the Royal Society for the Prevention of Cruelty to Animals (RSPCA) which was formed in 1864.

It was another campaigner on behalf of children, this time a woman, Eglantyne Jebb whose work, along with that of her sister, led to the creation of another major children's charity, Save the Children, and the idea of an international statement of children's rights. This developed the thinking of Ellen Key, a Swedish social reformer, who had written a book in 1900 called Century of the Child in which, 'she proposed that the world's children should be the central work of society during the twentieth century' (Koops and Zuckerman 2003, p. 10). Jebb drafted the Declaration of the Rights of Children, endorsed by the League of Nations General Assembly in 1924 and modified for adoption by the United Nations in 1946 and again 1953. Set against the 54 articles of the UNCRC the five statements listed below may seem modest but they were an important starting point for the formulation of the convention. What is interesting for our purposes is how closely they correspond with the five outcomes of the Children Act (2004).

1. The child must be given the means requisite for its normal development, both materially and spiritually.
2. The child that is hungry must be fed, the child that is sick must be nursed, the child that is backward must be helped, the delinquent child must be reclaimed, and the orphan and the waif must be sheltered and succoured.
3. The child must be the first to receive relief in times of distress.
4. The child must be put in a position to earn a livelihood, and must be protected against every form of exploitation.
5. The child must be brought up in the consciousness that its talents must be devoted to the service of its fellow man.

The Universal Declaration of Human Rights produced by the United Nations in1940 and adopted in 1948 applied to adults and children, but increasingly there was an acknowledgement of the need for a separate human rights instrument for children. The year 1959 saw the adoption of the second Declaration of the Rights of Children with its ten principles (Office of the High Commissioner for Human Rights). This was not legally binding but merely a statement of intent. It took ten years, beginning in 1979, to draft the United Nations Convention on the Rights of the Child (UNCRC) which became international law in 1990. The United Kingdom ratified the UNCRC in 1991 which means agreeing to work towards full implementation of the Articles with regular inspections by the Committee on the Rights of the child to evaluate and report on progress. Children in the United Kingdom are protected by The Human Rights Act (1998) which incorporates the rights enshrined in the European Convention on Human Rights.

Reflection

Article 43 states that governments should make children and young people aware of the convention and the rights it provides. In the last few years we have asked students at UWE whether they were introduced to their rights as set out in the Convention at any time during what is defined as their childhood. Without exception they have confirmed that the first time they became aware of it was during their first year of Early Childhood Studies which for many of them is the year they ceased to be children.

- What strategies should local and national government adopt to increase children's knowledge and understanding of UNCRC?

The true measure of a nation's standing is how well it attends to its children – their health and safety, their material security, their education and socialization, and their sense of being loved, valued, and included in the families and societies into which they are born. (UNICEF 2007, Report Card 7)

The key phrase for us in this statement is '*included in the families and societies into which they are born*'. Reviewing the myriad outcomes which have been designed *for* children, we are struck by how little consultation there is with the 'stakeholders' themselves, that is, children, and in particular young children. Although ECM and the Children's Plan refer to the inclusion of children in the planning and consultation a closer examination reveals the very small numbers involved.

You may ask how desirable and how practical it is to have increased participation by young children in decisions about their daily lives and learning experiences? At a curricula level there are impressive examples of young children determining their own agenda and flourishing as a result including

Susan Isaacs' Malting House experiment (1930), High/Scope, and Reggio Emilia. All of these are practical examples of respecting children and supporting their development through dialogue and humility. Each of these environments was built on a willingness to resist adult imposed outcomes. At a policy level there are fewer but Hallet and Prout (2003) include several examples in their book *Hearing the Voices of Children*.

Reflection

Each of the following websites have interactive children's pages seeking feedback from children regarding their experiences.

The Primary Review http://www.primaryreview.org.uk/Children/Childrenshomepage.html
The Good Childhood enquiry http://www.childrenssociety.org.uk/kids_zone/default.asp
Fair play consultation http://www.dcsf.gov.uk/playspace/
Visit at least two and compare with one of the four UK Children's Commissioners sites
Northern Ireland Commissioner for Children and Young People http://www.niccy.org/
Scotland Commissioner for Children and Young People http://www.sccyp.org.uk/
Children's Commissioner for Wales http://www.childcom.org.uk/index.php? lang=en
Children's Commissioner for England http://www.11million.org.uk/

Evaluate:
- How far you think they designed with the needs and interests of young children in mind? Note your reasons.
- How likely do you think children would be to use them?
- Is your answer the same if you think about children under 8 or under 5?
- How would you increase the number of responses?

In this chapter we've considered the expansion of government intervention in children's lives, the impact on families and some of the consequences for childhoods. If we revisit Bronfenbrenner's (1970) model, state intervention is drawing the focus away from the micro, that is, domestic, level to the macro level of government policy. The inclusion of children in the formulation of ideas and practices that affect them remains marginal. It is economic imperatives, linked with measures of accountability, which have dominated the development and implementation of an outcomes agenda. This in turn is predicated on a view of children as vulnerable and in need of extensive child protection measures. Children and childhood are reconstructed as social investments rather than social persons.

As Matthews (2007, p. 331) points out, we are uncertain what taking children seriously looks like.

The view that children are not full-fledged members of society is entrenched in cultures and institutions. The ramifications of organizing societies in which children have rights and determining what those rights might be are only beginning to be explored. The payoff for improving understanding of societies by including children and childhood seems worth the effort both for the field of sociology and the welfare of children.

Reflection

We would like to raise two important questions which you might like to use in your own evaluations of social policy affecting children.
- How far are early years settings, local authorities and central government prepared to include children younger than 8 years old in genuine consultation and participation?
- If children are not consulted how effective will policies focused on them be?

It would be wrong of us to end with anything other than the voices of children and we have chosen an example of children's inclusion in international policy making concerning their lives, specifically the importance of their participation in decision making which affects them. In 2002 the United Nations invited 404 children from across the globe to be delegates at the first ever Special Session for Children. The event included a three-day Children's Forum which culminated in the production of a statement delivered by two of the delegates to the General Assembly. The statement is called, 'A World fit for Us' (UNICEF website). Regarding the importance of consulting with children they expressed the following aspiration for a World fit for Children.

We see the active participation of children:
- raised awareness and respect among people of all ages about every child's right to full and meaningful participation, in the spirit of the Convention on the Rights of the Child,
- children actively involved in decision-making at all levels and in planning, implementing, monitoring and evaluating all matters affecting the rights of the child.

Summary
- The relationship between childhood experiences and the adults we become has been and remains significant.
- There has been a shift away from parents being responsible for providing for children towards government enacting this role.

Summary—Cont'd

- In aiming to provide the best for children policy makers have prescribed their experiences more and more tightly.
- A vital consideration for any analysis of policy directed towards children and childhood is whether they are imagined as 'beings' or 'becomings'.
- Parents are now included in the increasing regulation of children's experiences
- Children's rights have been evolved nationally and internationally in the last 100 years.
- There is a tension which exists between rhetoric exhorting us to listen to children and the tightening control and surveillance of their lives.
- Increased adherence to UNCRC requirement for children to be consulted in matters which concern them has the potential to reduce power imbalance between children and adults and strengthen mutual understanding and respect.

Recommended Reading

Rogoff, B. (2001) *The Cultural Nature of Human Development.* Oxford: Oxford University Press.

This book takes readers into the worlds of young children growing up in various contexts around the world. Rogoff explores the characteristics of these contexts and the behaviours observed in them as a way of understanding the impact of culture on children's development. Having read our chapter on ways in which children and their childhoods are being conceptualized in the United Kingdom currently, we suggest you explore what is happening in other parts of the world. This book is an excellent starting point.

Hallet, C. and Prout, A. (eds) (2003) *Hearing the Voices of Children: Social Policy for a New Century.* London: Routledge Falmer.

This book looks at both the *why* and *how* of involving children in the process of policy construction. The case for children as rights bearing citizens is vividly outlined. Declaring the UNCRC and European Human Rights legislation as its context it provides evidence that consulting with children about matters which affect their own lives is both desirable and practical. Contributors detail ways in which children have been engaged in policy. It provides valuable food for thought.

Clark, A., McQuail, S. and Moss, P. (2003) Exploring the field of consulting with and listening to young children. Research Report RR445 DCSF.

This report helps fill a space regarding the involvement of young children in decision making. It not only surveys existing practices but outlines Clark's innovative and important Mosaic Approach designed to support and validate the elicitation of children's experiences.

Bibliography

Anning, A. (2006) Early years education: mixed messages, in D. Kassem, E. Mufti, J.Robinson (eds) *Education Studies Issues and Critical Perspectives.* Maidenhead: Open University Press.

Bookstart Available at www.bookstart.org.uk [Accessed 14 May 2008].

Bowlby, J. (1953) *Childcare and the Growth of Love.* Baltimore: Pelican Books.

Bronfenbrenner, U. (1970) *Two Worlds of Childhood: US and USSR.* London: Allen and Unwin.

Buckingham, D. (2000). *After the Death of Childhood: Growing up in the Age of Electronic Media.* Cambridge: Polity Press.

Butcher, H. and Lee, J. (2008) Social Care, childcare and education, in P. Harnett (ed.) *Understanding Primary Education: Developing Professional Attributes, Knowledge and Skills.* Abingdon: Routledge.

Cameron, C. (2007) Understandings of care work with young children. Reflections on children's independence in a video observation study. *Childhood,* 14, 467–486.

Child Rights Information Network (CRIN) *Convention on the Rights of the Child.* Available at http://www.crin.org/resources/treaties/uncrc.asp#Twelve [Accessed 1 May 2008].

Clark, A., McQuail, S. and Moss., P. (2003) *Exploring the Field of Listening to and Consulting with Young Children.* Research Report 445. London: DfES.

Clark, A. and Statham, J. (2005) Listening to young children experts in their own lives, *Adoption and Fostering Journal,* 29, 1, 45–56 (12).

Committee on the Rights of the Child (CRC) (2002) Consideration of Reports Submitted by States Parties Under Article 44 of the Convention. *Concluding Observations of the Committee on the Rights of the Child: United Kingdom of Great Britain & Northern Ireland* CRC/C/Add.188.

Department for Children, Schools and Families (DCSF) (2007a), *Foundation Stage Profile Results in England, 2006/7.* Available online at: http://www.dcsf.gov.uk/rsgateway/DB/SFR/s000752/index.shtml [Accessed April 9 2009].

Department for Children, Schools and Families (DCSF) (2007b*) Time to Talk: Children's Plan Consultation 'Interim Summary Report of the Deliberative Event on 29/9/07'.* Available at http://www.dcsf.gov.uk/publications/childrensplan/timetotalk.shtml [Accessed 17 May 2008].

Department for Children, Schools and Families (DCSF) (2007c) *The Children's Plan: Building Brighter Futures.* London: TSO.

Department for Children, Schools and Families (DCSF) (2007d) *Every Parent Matters.* Available at: http://www.teachernet.gov.uk/_doc/11184/6937_DFES_Every_Parent_Matters_FINAL_PDF_as_published_130307.pdf [Accessed April 9 2009].

Department for Children, Schools and Families (DCSF) (2008), *Every Child Matters Outcomes Framework.* Available online at: http://www.dcsf.gov.uk/childrensplan/downloads/ECM%20outcomes%20framework.pdf [Accessed April 9 2009].

Department for Education and Employment (DfEE) (1998) *Meeting the Childcare Challenge.* Green Paper. London: HMSO.

Department for Education and Skills (DfES) (2002) *Birth to Three Matters: A Framework for Supporting Children in their Earliest Years.* London: DfES.

Department for Education and Skills (DfES) (2003) *Every Child Matters.* Green Paper. London: HMSO.

Department for Education and Skills (DfES) (2004) *Every Child Matters: Next Steps.* London: HMSO.

Department for Education and Skills (DfES) (2007) *The Early Years Foundation Stage: Setting the Standards for Learning Development and Care for Children from Birth to Five.* London: HMSO.

Dunn, J. (ed.) (1995) *Connections between Emotion and Understanding.* Hove: Lawrence Earlbaum.

Early Years Foundation Stage (2007) DfES. Nottingham: DfES Publications.

Edwards, A. & Warin, J. (1999) Parental involvement in raising the achievement of primary school pupils: why bother? *Oxford Review of Education* 25 (3), 325–341

Every Child Matters (2007) ContactPoint. Available at http://www.everychildmatters.gov.uk/contactpoint/ [Accessed April 9 2009].

Foundation Stage Profile (2006-07). *National Results.* Available at www.dcsf.gov.uk/rsgateway/DB/SFR [Accessed 9 June 2008].

The Good Childhood Inquiry. *About the Good Childhood Inquiry.* Available at http://www.childrenssociety.org.uk/all_about_us/how_we_do_it/thr_good_childhood_inquiry/about_the_good_childhood_inquiry/2254.html [Accessed 1 June 2008].

Gerhardt, S. (2004) *Why Love Matters.* Hove: Brunner Routledge.

Gopnik, A., Meltzoff, A. and Kuhl, P. (eds) (1999) *How Babies Think: The Science of Childhood.* London: Weidenfeld and Nicolson.

Hallet, C. and Prout, A. (eds) (2003) *Hearing the Voices of Children: Social Policy for a New Century.* London: Routledge Falmer.

Hallgarten, J. (2000) *Parents Matter OK!?* London: IPPR.

Hart, R. A. (1997) *Children's Participation in the Theory and Practice of Involving Young Citizens in Community Development and Environmental Care.* London: Earthscan.

Hendrick, H. (1997) Constructions and reconstructions of British childhood – an interpretative survey 1800 to the present, in A. James and A. Prout (eds) *Constructing and Reconstrucing Childhood: Contemporary Issues in the Sociological Study of Childhood.* London: Falmer.

HM Treasury (2001) *Tackling Child Property: Giving Every Child the Best Possible Start in Life.* A Pre-Budget report document. London: The Public Enquiry Unit.

Hohmann, M. and Weikart, D. (1995) *Educating Young Children; Active Learning Practices for Pre-school and Childcare Programmes.* Ypsilanti: High/Scope Press.

Hughes, M. (2002) *Learning in and out of school* Inaugural Lecture Bristol: University of Bristol.

Isaacs, S. (1930) *Intellectual Growth in Young Children.* London: Routledge and Sons.

Jenks, C. (1996) *Childhood.* London: Routledge.

Katz, L. (1992) Early childhood programs: multiple perspectives on quality. *Childhood Education,* Winter, 66–71.

Katz, Lilian G. (1994) The project approach. *ERIC Digest.* Champaign, IL: ERIC Clearinghouse on Elementary and Early Childhood Education. ED 368 509.

Koops, W. and Zuckerman, M. (eds) (2003) *Beyond the Century of the Child: Cultural History and Developmental Psychology.* Philidelphia: University of Pennsylvania Press.

Laming (2003) *The Victoria Climbie Inquiry Report of an Inquiry.* London: HMSO.

LeVine, R. A. (1988) Human parental care: universal goals, cultural strategies, individual behaviour, in R. A. LeVine, P. M. Miller and M. M. West (eds), *Parental Behaviour in Diverse Societies*. San Francisco: Jossey-Bass.

Levison, D. (2000) Children as economic agents, in *Feminist Economics*, 6, 1, 1 March, 125–134 (10).

Marsh, J. (2003) One-way traffic? Connections between literacy practices at home and in the nursery, *British Educational Research Journal*, 29, 3, 369–382.

Matthews, S. H. (2007) A window on the 'New' sociology of childhood, *Sociology Compass*, 1, 1, 322–334.

Mayall, B. (2007) *Children's Lives outside School and Their Educational Impact* (Primary Review Research Survey 8/1). Cambridge: University of Cambridge, Faculty of Education.

Montgomery, H., Burr, R. and Woodhead, M. (2003) *Changing Childhoods*. Chichester: Wiley.

Mooney, H. (2006) Junk culture killing childhood. in *The Guardian* 12 September 2006. Available at www.guardian.co.uk [Accessed 3 August 2008].

Muschamp, Y., Wikeley, F., Ridge, T. and Balarin, M. (2007) *Parenting, Caring and Educating* (Primary Review Research Survey 7/1) Cambridge: University of Cambridge, Faculty of Education.

National Children's Bureau (NCB) (1998) *Quality in Diversity in Early Learning: A Framework for Early Childhood Practitioners: a Collaborative Work*. London: NCB.

National Family and Parenting Institute. Available at www.nfpi.org.uk [Accessed on 16 April 2008].

The National Literacy Strategy framework for teaching (1998) DFEE.

Neuman, M. J. (2005) Governance of early childhood education and care, *Early Years: An International Journal of Research and Development*, 25, 2, 125–141.

NSPCC www.nspcc.org.uk/Inform/resourcesforprofessionals/InformationBriefings/childprotection-system_wda48949.html [Accessed on 23 March 2009].

Office of the High Commissioner for Human Rights Declaration on the Rights of the Child. Available at http://www.unhchr.ch/htm/menu3/b/25.htm [Accessed 16 May 2008].

Palmer, S. (2006) *Toxic Childhood: How the Modern World Is Damaging Our Children and What We Can Do about It*. London: Orion.

Parents Centre. Available at www.dfes.gov.uk/parentscentre [Accessed 2 June 2008].

The Primary Review (2006) *How Well Are We Doing? Research on Standards, Quality and Assessment in English Primary Education*. Cambridge: University of Cambridge.

Qualifications and Curriculum Agency (QCA) (2008) *Every Child Matters: at the heart of the curriculum*. Available online at: http://www.qca.org.uk/libraryAssets/media/ECM.pdf [Accessed April 9 2009].

Rabain Jamin, J. (1989) Culture and early social interactions: the example of mother-infant play in African and native French families in *European Journal of Psychology of Education*, 4, 295–305.

Reynolds, J. (2005) Parents' involvement in their children's learning and schools – How should their responsibilities relate to the role of the state? Policy Discussion Paper. London: Family & Parenting Institute.

Rinaldi, C. (2006) *In Dialogue with Reggio Emilia: Listening, Researching, and Learning*. London: Routledge.

Rogoff, B. (2001) *The Cultural Nature of Human Development*. Oxford: Oxford University Press.

Sameroff, A. (1987) The social context of development, in N. Eisenberg (ed.) *Contemporary Topics in Developmental Psychology*. New York: Wiley.

School Curriculum and Assessment Authority (SCAA) (1996) *Desirable Outcomes for Children's Learning on Entering Compulsory Education*. London: HMSO.

Tizard, B. (1991) Working mothers and the care of young children, in E. Lloyd and A.Phoenix (eds) *Social Construction of Motherhood*. London: Sage.

UNICEF (2002) *United Nations Special Session on Children 'A World Fit for Us'* Available at http://www.unicef.org/specialsession/child_participation/fit_for_us.html [Accessed 15 May 2008].

UNICEF (2007) Report Card 7. *An Overview of Child Wellbeing in Rich Countries*. Available from: http://www.unicef-irc.org/publications/pdf/rc7_eng.pdf [Accessed 9 June 2008].

Vincent, C. with Stephen Ball, S. (2005) The childcare champion? New Labour, social justice and the childcare market, in *British Educational Research Journal*, 31, 5, 557–570.

Warin, J. and Edwards A. (1999) Parental involvement in raising the achievement of primary school pupils: why bother? in *Oxford Review of Education*; 25, 3, 325–341.

Williams, F. (1989) *Social Policy: A Critical Introduction. Issues of Race, Gender and Class*. Cambridge: Polity.

Earlier and Earlier to School?

Christine Screech

This chapter introduces you to the notion of curriculum. Through a historical contextualization, current trends in early years UK curricula will be considered and alternative perspectives and particular approaches to teaching and learning will be explored.

Key Questions

1. Where do early years curricula come from?
2. How are children represented within this provision?

Curriculum

Mick Waters, current Director of Curriculum for QCA, appears uncompromisingly clear about what our response to the 'learning that the nation has decided to set before its young' or the 'curriculum' should be:

The curriculum should be treasured. There should be real pride in our curriculum: the learning that the nation has decided to set before its young. Teachers, parents, employers, the media and the public should all see the curriculum as something to embrace, support and celebrate. Most of all, young people should relish the opportunity for discovery and achievement that the curriculum offers. (Waters 2008)

Perhaps, as you read this statement you may be surprised by the rather mixed messages that are evident. On the one hand, you may note a somewhat didactic approach, and yet this is coupled with an acknowledgement at least of experiential, discovery learning. In tandem with the statement above, you should consider the reflective activity below which asks you to explore QCA's 'A Big Picture of the Curriculum' (QCA 2008). When taken together these reflect some of the many paradoxes of current UK curriculumization and it is consideration of these, particularly as they relate to the teaching, learning and lives of our youngest children that will be investigated in this chapter.

Reflection

Access QCA's 'A Big Picture of the Curriculum' – available at: http://www.qca.org.uk/libraryAssets/media/Big_Picture_2008.pdf

1. What do you think this model is trying to express?
2. How effectively do you think it represents the teaching and learning needs of our youngest children?

Reflection

Access *A Curriculum for the 21st Century* from which Mick Water's (Director of Curriculum for QCA) statement on curriculum outlined above is taken – available at: http://www.nga.org.uk/uploads/QCA%20Supplement.pdf

1. Why do you think there is no acknowledgement in this document of the existence of a 'curriculum' for children below KS1?
2. Do you think this is a significant omission?

Of course, whatever your reflections on curriculum from considering the models and questions above, it is worth remembering that international, comparative research (Schweinhart et al. 1986; West and Varlaam 1990; Bertram and Pascal 2002) suggests that we are currently getting it wrong and that although children in the United Kingdom may be 'ahead' (and, of course, this in itself is a subjective term) by the age of 6, Finnish children, for example, who do not begin formal education until the age of 7, outperform all other nations in reading, mathematical and science literacy by the age of 15. In other words the validity of an earlier and earlier curriculum is not substantiated by evidence and yet there continues to be an imperative to advance curriculumization towards ever younger children, culminating, of course, in September 2008 with the introduction of the Early Years Foundation Stage, which provides a statutory framework encompassing learning, development and care from birth itself. You may wish to ask yourself, in the light of this, what drives the burgeoning amount of English legislation for our youngest children given that in other parts of the United Kingdom, Wales for example, cognizance has clearly been taken of the research evidence resulting in the instigation of a distinct play based foundation phase for children between the ages of 3 and 7, ensuring that formal education does not begin until children reach Key Stage 2 at age 7.

Reflection

From reading the paragraph above, you will be aware of the research evidence suggesting that non-formalized approaches to early years education are valid.

1. Why do you think the Early Years Foundation Stage has become the chosen option here?
2. What do you think are the imperatives that drive us towards earlier and earlier curriculization? Whose imperatives are they?

Of course, you may find that your reflections on these questions are less than palatable and led by agendas quite different to those that you initially expected. As you will notice from reading later parts of this chapter, the English education system is driven by a standards agenda that focuses heavily on the outcomes of learning rather than on the process and experience through which children acquire their understanding. This top-down pressure imposed through regimes of statutory testing, regular OFSTED visits and local and national league tables inevitably decrees that classrooms become less child-centred and more target driven. In the recent past , for example, you may have noted the emphasis on promoting earlier and earlier approaches to reading and writing based ostensibly on the findings of the Independent Review of the teaching of early reading (Rose Review, DfES 2006). But, given that we now know from research evidence that this very early intervention will pay few or no dividends in the long run, to whose advantage is this? What it does provide, of course, is evidence for OFSTED that there is a focus on raising standards;

possibly, the SATs levels in some schools will rise, at least temporarily; possibly the national league tables of children achieving Level 4 or above at age 11 will move a couple of percentage points upwards, so government statistics will appear more promising. Represented somewhere within this rather cynical picture is 'the child', and yet you may feel that they have become little more than pawns in the game that we call education, their lives and their needs becoming almost subsumed by the other agendas described, placed within a regulatory agenda designed to give the adults and policy makers control of their lives. You may consider that the Early Years Foundation stage with its *statutory* requirements for learning, development and welfare and associated practice guidance for *all* settings moves yet another step further in prioritizing government agendas at the expense of children and children's lives. Perhaps, then, as you read this chapter, and indeed, whenever you encounter policy or curricula in practice, you need to consider not only whose agenda is prioritized but also, as the title of this book suggests, whose childhood is it anyway?

Looking back and learning from *Plowden*

The idea of a curriculum applicable to the needs of young children is by no means new and successive governments have striven to make their own mark on the education of young children. Of course, elements of past curriculum and pedagogy become re-conceptualized and transformed over time and as you approach more recent documentation, it is useful to have an awareness of the ways in which earlier policy has impacted upon it. A good example of this is The Plowden Report (CACE 1967), in that much of its empirically gathered research base correlates quite directly with the *Principles of Early Years Education* set out in the *Curriculum Guidance for the Foundation Stage* (DfEE/QCA 2000, p. 11).

The Plowden Report, for example, is clear that 'one of the main educational tasks of the primary school is to build on and strengthen children's *intrinsic* interest in learning and lead them to learn for themselves rather than from fear of disapproval or desire for praise' (CACE 1967, p. 47). You may also consider the report to be ahead of its time, in that it did not presume a canon of knowledge to be learned but advocated a thematic approach in which the curriculum emanated from the child's previous knowledge and interests rather than a top-down model imposed externally. Building on existing knowledge also, of course, implies building on what children bring with them from their home backgrounds and the report dedicates a whole section to *Home, School and Neighbourhood*. Parents as children's 'first and most enduring educators' (Riley 2003, p. 151) has become a constant and salient mantra of early years pedagogy and curriculum and an awareness of the positive impact on development and learning when parents and practitioners work together in early years settings (DfEE/QCA 2000; DfES 2004) has now become firmly embedded into foundation stage practice.

There are several themes that seem to constantly recur throughout the report, namely, the idea of the uniqueness of each child and their learning; flexibility in the curriculum; use of the environment; active learning and holistic evaluation of children's progress. However, perhaps most significant in terms of establishing an early years ethos is the style of learning, espoused by the report and exemplified by the extract below:

> The children seem to be using every bit of the building (the top floor is sealed off) and its surroundings. They spread into the hall, the corridors and the playground. The nursery class has its own quarters and the children are playing with sand, water, paint, clay, dolls, rocking horses and big push toys under the supervision of their teacher. This is how they learn. There is serenity in the room, belying the belief that happy children are always noisy. The children make rather a mess of themselves and their room, but this, with a little help, they clear up themselves. A dispute between two little boys about who is to play with what is resolved by the teacher and a first lesson in taking turns is learned. Learning is going on all the time, but there is not much direct teaching. (CACE 1967, p. 278)

Reflection

1. How would you describe what is going on in the extract above?
2. Do you notice anything about the tone of this extract when compared with Mick Water's description of curriculum on p. 1?

The above extract clearly exhibits Bruce's description of children being allowed to 'wallow in their learning' (Bruce 2001, p. 24) and traditionally play, particularly the type of 'free-play' that we observe here, has been seen as the medium for such opportunities. You may have noted that the final sentence suggests that children are learning from their play, although the adult is purely in the role of 'supervisor' and there is 'not much direct teaching'; in other words although the play you observe appears to be entirely child initiated as opposed to teacher-led, a range of both cognitive and intellectual skills are clearly being developed – motivation, problem-solving, self-direction, engagement, concentration, negotiation and collaboration to name but a few!

Of course, the type of play exemplified by the observation from *Plowden* above might not be quite that envisaged by the *Curriculum Guidance for the Foundation* Stage, where classroom play is characterized as being 'well planned' and 'purposeful' (DfEE/QCA 2000, p. 15); the type of play Hutt et al. (1979) describe as 'epistemic' or in Moyles' terms, 'a tool for learning' (2005, p. 94) and, indeed, one of the realities of classroom play today is that it is often mistrusted and not viewed as being 'real work' for children unless it is teacher-directed with a clear objective and measurable outcome.

The idea of mistrust is one that was squarely levelled at *Plowden* and it may be argued that the prescription of the National Curriculum and the resultant requirement for a separate foundation stage stems indirectly from this source. For example, in the following transcript, you see Professor Michael Barber of the *Primary National Strategy* speaking of the era left in its wake:

> around the time of the Plowden Report in 1967, that era was overthrown – rightly – because it was deeply inequitable. It was replaced by an era of professional control and informality, which dominated the next 20 years. Even in the very good schools, and there were many, professional control became axiomatic. Into the core of the culture of the teaching profession was built the concept that it was up to each teacher in each classroom to both design the curriculum and decide the methodology. That's what I did in my classroom in the late 70s and early 80s, and what happened to standards? Nothing. And what happened to equity? Hindsight is a wonderful thing, and we can see now that this outcome was inevitable. How could it possibly have been otherwise? Where was the systematic sharing of knowledge? Individuals can learn, and did, but the system was unable to . . .
> (Barber 2004)

It may be suggested that it is Barber's notion of 'professional control' that the National Curriculum had the effect of summarily sweeping away from primary classrooms. For those working with the youngest children, the *Curriculum Guidance for the Foundation Stage* seemed once again to herald the return of the professional judgement of the practitioner and the very language of the foundation stage documentation itself initially appears less didactic and more measured than that of the National Curriculum. If you consider, for example, the first report of the Select Committee on Education and Employment, it states that it supports the 'QCA's *Curriculum Guidance for the Foundation*

Stage which *illustrates* rather than *imposes* stepping stones for a child to progress from the age of three to the end of the foundation stage' and recognizes 'the scale of challenge' that requires 'practitioners with *imagination* and *flexibility* to enable children to learn in ways appropriate to their development' (UK Parliament 2001). Elizabeth Wood summarizes very concisely the perceived strengths and weaknesses of *Plowden* in the extract below:

> The Plowden Report had a significant impact on early childhood education, because it reified developmental theories, and child-centred approaches to learning through discovery, exploration and play, and to planning the curriculum around children's needs and interests. However, these constructs proved to be problematic in theory and in practice, and provoked unprecedented policy interventions in curriculum and pedagogy. (Wood 2007, Abstract)

Of course, it is worth remembering that *Plowden* was not aimed at children below the age of 5 and the early years principles that we find bound up within it were very much aimed at children within primary schools. So, how did the vast swathes of policy that followed in the wake of Plowden move us towards earlier and earlier curriculumlization that with the implementation of the Early Years Foundation Stage in September 2008, provides us with one framework of guidance that starts from birth itself?

From Rumbold to the foundation stage

It was the Thatcher government of the early 1980s that first introduced wholesale changes that would sweep through education over the next 20 years with the 1981 document *The School Curriculum,* taking as its opening mantra the phrase, 'the school curriculum is at the heart of education' (DES 1981). As the decade moved forward, the Education Reform Act of 1988 heralded the introduction of The National Curriculum into England, Wales and Northern Ireland as nationwide, statutory curriculum provision for all state primary and secondary schools and with it a model of centralized teaching based on subject related programmes of study, attainment targets and a formalized testing regime for children as young as 7, became a reality. In 1989, the UN Convention on the Rights of the Child, a universally agreed set of non-negotiable standards, principles and obligations to safeguard the human rights and best interests of children across the world was ratified. As you compare the two statements below, the first from the UN Convention, the second from the Education Reform Act, you may at first be surprised to discover the similarities between the two:

Reflection

Compare the following statements: -

UN Convention on the Rights of the Child – Article 29
The Education of the child shall be directed to:

> development of the child's personality, talents and mental and physical abilities to their fullest potential. (UN 1989)

Education Reform Act, 1988
> *The curriculum must promote 'the spiritual, moral cultural, mental, physical development of pupils . . . and prepare pupils for the opportunities, responsibilities and experiences of adult life. (UK Parliament 1988)*

1. What do you think are the key differences between these statements?
2. Is the word 'pupils' significant?

However, perhaps it is the key differences that give us the greatest indication of the representation of children at the heart of National Curriculum documentation. First, you may notice that the UN Convention uses the word 'child'; the Education Reform Act refers to 'pupils'. Although you may see this as a minor nuance, a dictionary search may alert you to some quite different connotations. The term 'pupil' is very much based on behaviourist principles of learning where the adult takes control of the teaching and the 'pupil' is the empty vessel passively waiting to be filled with knowledge. You may also note that the Education Reform Act views a curriculum as preparation for adult life, an approach that Nutbrown refers to as the 'adult-in-waiting construction of childhood'. She further suggests that:

> The 'adults in waiting' construction of childhood devalues children as capable learners. It underpins the creation of narrow curricula and systems of educating which are built on the transmission of pre-ordained, pre-packed nuggets of knowledge. Such perspectives on childhood omit children who can use their powers

as thinkers from the learning equation and, too often, denies their humanity. (Nutbrown 2000)

Once again, of course, the curriculum under discussion was aimed at children above the age of 5 and, under the remit of the National Curriculum, beginning compulsory education in Key Stage 1. However, in 1990, just as the new National Curriculum was being rolled out in primary schools, a new Government report, *Starting with Quality: The Report of the Committee of Inquiry into the Quality of the Educational Experience Offered to 3 and 4 year olds.* (The Rumbold Report, DES 1990) was published. Once again, this report may be viewed as a significant catalyst for reform of both early years policy and practice given that it suggested that, in contrast to the National Curriculum, the *context* of learning and the *process* of learning should be valued in equal measure to the content of learning:

Children are affected by the context in which learning takes place, the people involved in it, and the values and beliefs which are embedded in it. For the early years educator, therefore, the process of education – how children are encouraged to learn – is as important as, and inseparable from, the content – what they learn. We believe that this principle must underlie all curriculum planning for the under fives. (DES 1990, p. 8)

The report did not however exclude the notion of curriculum and although a 'National Curriculum' for children aged 3 and 4 was not advocated, a 'flexible framework from which a curriculum can be developed to suit the needs of individual children in a variety of settings' (DES 1990, p. 9), was proposed and six areas of learning around which the framework might be constructed were recommended. Throughout the 1990s a plethora of additional guidance in support of the teaching and learning of 3 and 4 year-olds was produced by the School Curriculum and Assessment Authority (SCAA); perhaps the most significant of these being *The Desirable Learning Outcomes* (1996) providing, for the first time, a set of assessment indicators outlining what children should be expected to 'know, understand and do' by the age of 5 in each of the six 'curriculum areas'. A consultation on the Desirable Learning Outcomes and proposals for curriculum guidance for a distinct stage of education from the age of 3 to the end of the reception year was carried out in 1999, culminating in October 1999 with publication of the *Early Learning Goals* to replace the desirable learning outcomes as an assessment tool for the foundation stage. Further guidance followed in May 2000 with the publication of *Curriculum Guidance for the Foundation Stage* which contained information on six areas of learning, each with stepping stones and early learning goals. It also included principles for early years education, and advice for practitioners on teaching, learning, planning and assessment. The *Curriculum Guidance for the Foundation Stage* became the core reference document for the foundation stage from September 2000 with the introduction of a new national assessment scheme for the foundation stage, *The Foundation Stage Profile,* in 2001.

This early emphasis on assessment of 3 and 4 year-olds may, of course, be construed from a number of different perspectives. If you are a nursery or reception teacher, you may consider that collecting initial data on children's educational achievement is valuable in that it allows for appropriate early intervention and hence progression; a head teacher may use the data as an evaluative measure of the effectiveness of her foundation stage provision. However, you should also consider whether it indicates a particular construction of early childhood that is broadly developed to fit the prevailing socio-political context and where an effective early years curriculum is viewed as yielding 'an important economic bonus in the long term' (Jowett and Sylva 1986, p. 46). In contrast, New Zealand, Spain, Sweden and Switzerland (Bertram and Pascal 2002), place no focus at all on academic learning in their early years provision but choose instead to prioritize children's social and emotional capacities and learning dispositions. The New Zealand early years curriculum, *Te Whariki,* specifically focuses upon the principle of empowerment, as does the *Reggio-Emilio* approach in Northern Italy that constructs an image of the child as 'rich strong and powerful' (Edwards et al. 1993, p. 38). If, however, you do consider that socio-economic indicators impact on the view of early childhood espoused by our UK early years curriculum, it is little wonder that in national and international comparisons England is one of a very limited number of countries that has a national system of assessment across all forms of funded early educational provision and is the only identifiable country to use assessment data as an evaluative baseline measure for subsequent school performance (Bertram and Pascal 2002). This is in direct contrast to Sweden and France who view the formal assessments of pre-school children as premature and potentially harmful.

You might also find it intriguing to speculate on the notion of play promulgated by this so-called 'play based' curriculum. The *Curriculum Guidance for the Foundation Stage* contains a huge number of references to play and to play based learning. Indeed, one whole page of the documentation sets out to describe the type of play that it envisages:

> Well-planned play, both indoors and outdoors, is a key way in which young children learn with enjoyment and challenge. In playing, they behave in different ways: sometimes their play will be boisterous, sometimes they will describe and discuss what they are doing, sometimes they will be quiet and reflective as they play. (DfEE/QCA 2000, p. 26)

Throughout the documentation, there are numerous uses of the word 'planned' and 'structured' and indeed the nature of the documentation is delineated quite clearly within Margaret Hodge's introduction by references to what 'might reasonably be *expected* of children in the foundation stage' and her assertion that 'the principal aim of the documentation is to help practitioners to *plan how their work will contribute to the achievement of the early learning goals*' (Ibid 2000, p. 3). If you acknowledge that the notion of child-centred play is built on a belief that the play fits the child, rather than the child fitting the play, then you are immediately faced with a curious dichotomy here between the *Principles for Early Years Education* that underpin the foundation stage curriculum and the rhetoric of the documentation itself. Of course, it may be that practitioners' interpretations of what constitutes 'play' are more in line with the curriculum documentation than the principles – it would be a rare foundation stage classroom in my experience that encourages truly boisterous play and by Y1 such play becomes all but invisible except in the playground. Abbots and Rogers (1994) have described child-centeredness as 'being where the child is at' and allowing the play to flow from that starting point. They cite examples from Sweden which suggest that adults' and children's perceptions of what constitute play can and do differ and yet there appears to be little cognizance of children's perspectives of play, or indeed of their voice more generally, in the development of the *Curriculum Guidance for the Foundation Stage.*

Fundamentally then, although you might consider this documentation to be underpinned by a set of well-meaning principles, there seems to have been little attempt before its inception to discuss the many complex arguments surrounding what early childhood education is *for* and whose wishes and needs are given priority within it. If, as Soler and Miller (2003) suggest, our views on early childhood are implicitly expressed through the curriculum we offer, then it is little wonder that early years curricula may be viewed as peren-nial 'sites of struggle' (Ibid 2003, p. 24).

Birth to Three Matters to the Early Years Foundation Stage

However, this trend towards ever greater curriculumization for ever younger children did not stop with the creation of the foundation stage. With the expan-sion of childcare identified in the National Childcare Strategy and the Green Paper (DfEE 2001), there came a growing recognition that it was children's earliest experiences that were most influential in shaping the pattern of their adult life and to support this very early development, *Birth to Three Matters – A Framework to Support Children in Their Earliest Years* (Sure Start 2002) was created, implementing a framework of provision for children from birth itself for the very first time, billed and, indeed villified in the media as a 'curriculum for babies'.

Reflection

Access *Birth to Three Matters* at: http://www.standards.dfes.gov.uk/primary/publications/foundation_stage/940463/ss_birth2_3matters_birth.pdf

1. Read the Foreword on page 3. What do you see as the main aims of this guidance?
2. As you read through, do some of the precepts seems familiar to you? Can you detect where they come from?

Of course, you might think it is arguable whether legislating for the experi-ences of the youngest children is a valid way of promoting their best interests and taking into account the imperatives for implementing provision discussed at the beginning of the chapter, you may be suspicious of government inten-tions, but nevertheless, here we have a set of guidance that purports to:

> take as its focus the child and steers away from subjects, specific areas of experience and distinct curriculum headings. It identifies four Aspects, which celebrate the skill and competence of babies and young children and highlights the interrelationship between growth, learning, development and the environ-ment in which they are cared for and educated. (Sure Start 2002, p. 5)

These four 'Aspects' are:

1. A Strong Child
2. A Skilful Communicator
3. A Competent Learner
4. A Healthy Child

Furthermore it is underpinned by a very substantial literature review compiled by a team of reflective, influential early years exponents (David et al. 2002), that, drawing on the work of Goldschmied and Jackson (1994) represents 'people under three, not babies, toddlers or even children, but people with rights, which include being treated with dignity and respect'. Of course, once again, if you re-examine earlier documentation you may again find parallels, but you may notice here that similarities, at least at first glance, are most closely drawn with *Te Whariki*, the early childhood curriculum in New Zealand and its aspiration for all children:

> to grow up as competent and confident learners and communicators, healthy in mind, body, and spirit, secure in their sense of belonging and in the knowledge that they make a valued contribution to society. (NZ Ministry of Education 1996)

The New Zealand early years curriculum, *Te Whariki*, Maori for woven mat, seeks to draw together holistically the many threads of children's lives to provide a coherent bi-lingual, socio-cultural framework for their learning and development. However, also permeating throughout *Te Whariki* is a construct of childhood based on the Maori principle of '*empowering* children to learn and grow' and it is this acknowledgement of children's rights, their strength and their competence, that we begin to see reflected for the first time in English curriculum documentation when we explore *Birth to Three Matters*, albeit at a rather fledgling level.

Reflection

Before reading the next section you might like to watch:

Teachers' TV - School Matters, Early Years Foundation Stage
Available at: http://www.teachers.tv/video/19765

- How far do you agree with the views put forward on the programme?
- Do you think that co-ordinating and unifying a child's education and welfare from birth to the age of 5 is a good idea?

Although, as you will have noted from reading the chapter so far, the delivery of early years teaching and learning had never slipped far from the government's radar over the past decade, you may regard 2003 as a particularly significant turning point in that the Green Paper, *Every Child Matters*, was published alongside the formal response to the report into the death of Victoria Climbié, and services for children, young people and families moved inexorably to the centre of government agendas. The ten year childcare strategy, *Choice for Parents the Best Start for Children* published on 2 December 2004 (DES 2004a) set out new policy initiatives designed to give every child 'the best start in life' and signalled an intention to develop a single quality framework to address the integrated needs of children from birth to the August after their fifth birthday – the Early Years Foundation Stage. Building on the objectives of the 2003 Green Paper, *Every Child Matters*, its much acclaimed aim was to put children and childhood at the centre of policy making and delivery at both local and national level and thus to improve over a ten-year period the life chances of all children.

Building on the existing Birth to Three Matters Framework, the Curriculum Guidance for the Foundation Stage and the National Standards for Under 8s Day Care and Childminding, the Early Years Foundation Stage brought together guidance related to children's welfare, learning and development underpinned by the five outcomes of Every Child Matters:

1. Be healthy
2. Stay safe
3. Enjoy and achieve
4. Make a positive contribution
5. Achieve economic well-being

As you read through these outcomes it may strike you that one is pretty hard to measure and has proved impossible to legislate for and is thus likely to quietly slip down the priority list. A brief scan of much official documentation will indicate that enjoyment is always linked with achievement against official targets and is linked to age and subject content.

It is arguable whether the Early Years Foundation Stage framework can in the truest sense of the word be called a curriculum, in that its agenda is not solely around learning but to integrate 'learning, development and care from birth to five' (DfES 2007, p. 5). However, again, it is underpinned by a set of principles designed to guide the work of all early years practitioners and these are grouped into four themes:

1. A Unique Child
2. Positive Relationships
3. Enabling Environments
4. Learning and Development

You may note that the principle of a 'unique child' builds once again on both the Reggio Emilia and *Te Whariki* approaches to suggest that 'every child is a competent learner from birth who can be resilient, capable, confident and self-assured' (DfES 2007, p. 5). However, the framework stops short of the term 'empowerment' and with it any assumption of children's rights. There is an acknowledgement (p. 9) of sustained shared thinking where 'adults and children work together to develop an idea or skill' but once again the visibility of children's voice and an acknowledgement of children as co-constructors of meaning and experts in their own lives is not perceptible. The Council of Europe's Commissioner for Human Rights, Thomas Hammarberg summarizes effectively the reasons why successive governments continue to remain non-compliant with Article 12 of the UN Convention on the Rights of the Child that places an obligation on them to ensure that children's views are sought and considered on all matters that affect their lives:

> The objective should be to create a culture of greater receptivity to and respect for children's views. Unfortunately many adults seem to consider this prospect a threat. The issue of children's influence is seen as a 'zero-sum gain' – that is, a situation in which one side wins only if the other side loses. In other words, if children get more power, adults believe they will lose some of theirs and be less able to control the family, or uphold discipline in the classroom. (Hammarberg 2007)

Interestingly, the underpinning pedagogical principles of the *Children's Workforce Development Council* that inform the training of those gaining *Early Years Professional* status does appear to be moving further forward – the child being constructed here as a 'complex social being with rich and extraordinary potential, rather than as an adult in waiting' and an acknowledgement of the importance of seeing the child within 'their own life world' (CWDC 2006). Let us hope that in time, this is representative of the discourse and values that will begin to permeate not only the *Early Years Foundation Stage* but KS1, too.

Of course, you may feel that this is benign, statutory documentation designed to improve the life chances of all children and that the discourse of the documentation is of less importance than the policy within. Certainly if you compare, for example the views of the NSPCC with those of the Independent Schools Council, you may feel that this is a framework of guidance designed to iron out inequality and to ensure that all children have equal access to high quality early years provision.

Reflection

NSPCC

The early years are a crucial stage in children's learning and development. The Effective Provision of Pre-school Education (EPPE) has shown that attending pre-school has an important impact on a child's development. Disadvantaged children in particular can benefit significantly from good quality pre-school experiences. Care cannot be considered to be of good quality unless it provides opportunities for children to learn and develop. However, learning cannot be considered to be of good quality unless it is provided within an environment where all children feel safe, secure and included. (NSPCC 2006, p. 2)

Independent Schools Council

By definition independent schools have the freedom to set their own curriculum and have freedom in their choice of pupils and are not dependent on Government or Local Authority finance. Why then are they now being told that they will need to adhere to the Early Years Foundation Stage (EYFS) and be inspected by OFSTED for their under-5? These restrictions undermine the very route of success of independent schools, which rely on their freedom from regulation by central and local government and also of each other. Excessive bureaucratic burden of assessment associated with extensive form-filling creates no tangible benefit to children, and results in the diversion of teacher time from more beneficial tasks. There is also the imposition of staff qualification requirements on the independent sector that EYFS brings. Is it also not a violation of parents' rights, who select independent schools because of their independence? Children who are particularly able are likely to be held back by the implementation of these regulations and therefore will not receive the support they need. (ISC 2008)

1. Why do you think these perspectives on the Early Years Foundation Stage are so different?
2. Do you think there is any justification in the view of the Independent Schools Council or is this just 'sour grapes'?

But if you do consider the Early Years Foundation Stage a lost opportunity in terms of establishing children's right to stronger visibility and voice, you may also consider that by establishing an arbitrary cut-off point of 5 years old it effectively continues to marginalize Year 1 and Year 2 children by planting them squarely back into the confines of the National Curriculum at Key Stage 1. It might also be viewed therefore as a wasted opportunity to address the real concerns surrounding the onset of formal teaching, which, as we have already noted at the beginning of the chapter, research suggests has very limited benefit until around the age of 7. The development of the new birth to five framework provided the DfES with a real opportunity to be cognizant of this in their planning and to establish a truly integrated approach to principles, pedagogy and practice from birth to seven. However, in spite of research evidence it seems that this remained too radical a step and transition, continuity and coherence is summarily distilled into one paragraph of the framework (p. 10) with an acknowledgement that 'a high quality early years experience provides a firm foundation on which to build future academic, social and emotional success' (DfES, 2007: 10).

Into Key Stage 1

So far in the chapter we have considered primarily the curriculumization of children from birth to the end of the reception year. However, as children reach 5, they begin their next curriculum journey, this time into compulsory education and the beginning of Key Stage 1 where they first encounter the National Curriculum. As we have already seen through our exploration of *Plowden*, the education of children between the ages of 5 and 7 (or indeed further up in the school) has not always been curricularized into subject areas with prescribed teaching content in the way it is today and over the past few years there has been a considerable body of research (DfES/Sure Start 2004; Sanders et al. 2005) suggesting that continuity of practice between the foundation stage and Y1 constitutes vital and key elements of effective early years teaching and learning. OFSTED's report, *Transition from the Reception Year to Year 1*, for example, stated that: -

> Nationally, insufficient consideration has been given to the relationship between the areas of learning in the foundation stage and the subjects of the National

Curriculum in Year 1. The subject-based approach of the National Curriculum has been interpreted sensitively by many Year 1 teachers. However, constraints of timetabling and the need to make sure that pupils make good progress towards the standards expected in the national end of Key Stage 1 tests some-times lead to abrupt transitions to more formal approaches in Year 1. (OfSTED 2004, p. 5)

An additional advocate of the cause was David Bell, ex-Chief Inspector of Schools, whose submission that 'children in key stage 1 are often quite unhappy with the formal didactic transmission model approach' and that 'children don't enjoy school in the way we know they can' (Bell 2003, p. 3) taken in conjunc-tion with Bruce's contention that in the early years the brain is 'geared up' to language and play and that our current KS1 teaching 'closes down learning' (Bruce 2005, p. 47), provided further evidence that the National Curriculum does not satisfactorily address children's needs.

As a reflective practitioner I am sure that you are constantly aware that 'education is inevitably concerned not just with what is, but also with what ought to be' (Pollard 2002, p. 59), but making any aspiration become reality inevitably raises many issues. In *TES Staffroom*, for example, one Y1 teacher (accompanied by many others) affirms this:

'it just seems to make the planning terribly complicated, confusing and difficult and how do you provide a foundation stage-type setting in an ordinary, small classroom with little adult help and the remaining statutory demands for a subject based national curriculum?' (Hepplewhite 2005, p. 2).

However, if we consider that in some parts of the United Kingdom, Wales, for example, the dilemma of addressing tensions between two variant stages and models of practice has been overcome by the introduction of a play-based foundation phase curriculum for all 3 to 7 year-olds, then we have clear evidence that there are accessible ways of moving forward. If we also accept that 'at its best, the management of transition from the reception year to Year 1 is part of a broader whole school approach to achieving good curricular continuity and progression in pupils' learning' (DfES/QCA 2000) then we might envisage YR/Y1 transition as a vehicle through which whole-school improvement might be managed as well as a means of ensuring that children move forward with 'their enthusiasm maintained, their wonder increased and their self esteem intact' (Featherstone 2005).

So, where does this leave Y1 classrooms and Y1 teachers now? Lesley Staggs, when National Director of the Foundation Stage of the *Primary National Strategy*, stated that 'instead of making reception classes more like Y1, we should be making Y1 more like reception' (Staggs 2005, p. 14), and, in support of this sentiment, in the autumn term of 2005, all primary schools received a training pack, *Continuing the Learning Journey* (QCA/Primary National Strategy 2005) designed to establish a shared understanding of the principles of the foundation stage as well as promoting best practice for transition between foundation stage and Year 1. The following excerpt describes two boys' concerns about their experience in year one; there are, of course, a number of ways in which smoother transitions can be encouraged:

Reflection

Researcher:	Is there anything you don't like about being in Year 1?
First Boy:	Being on the carpet for a long time.
Second Boy:	Neither do I because it's very boring.
First Boy:	And it wastes our time playing.
Second Boy:	It wastes your life. (Sanders et al, 2005)

1. From reading the views of the Y1 children in the excerpt above, what do you think might be the significant change/s between the foundation stage and Key Stage 1 curriculum?
2. Can you identify any ways in which the transition between stages and Curricula could be mediated to give children a better experience?

Although the foundation stage curriculum offers opportunities predominantly for adult-led, structured play which is outcome driven, nevertheless one of its founding principles is that 'play underpins the delivery of all the EYFS' (DfES 2007, p. 7) and it is this sentiment that children seem to value and fear losing most as they meet Year 1 particularly as it implies an active, hands-on learning style that has been seen to match the preferred kinaesthetic learning styles of many 5- and 6-year-old boys. The following illustration comes from Year 1 children who were invited to photograph and then annotate what they liked best about Year 1. Both boys express this effectively, albeit with a slight air of wistfulness for their time in reception classes!

Matthew – Year 1

When we went to the farm, we saw animals and we played outside. I liked going there but I didn't like having to do work about it when we came back. I like it when we go outside. In reception we had more things outside. Now we've got a little bit but we have to work and not go there much.

Jake – Year 1

I like it when we make things. I really wanted to take that teddy home to show my mum but she had to come in and see it on the wall. I made one when I got home but I didn't have any of those, those . . . things to put it together (split pins). I like all the making things we do in Year 1. These were tricky but they do end up like teddy bears. In reception, sometimes, cos' we couldn't do things, they didn't come out right.

However, while ensuring that Year 1 follows in the footsteps of what has gone before might ease children's transition between 2 stages of learning, have children already by the age of 5, become encultured into what might be described as the rather passive and compliant practices of a school community, described by Crook (2001) as the 'contrived agendas of school life'?

If we accept Bourdieu's theory of cultural capital (cited in Robinson and Jones Diaz 2006) that children whose home and cultural practices are congruent with the pedagogical practices of the schools are most likely to experience academic success, then for particular groups of children it may be that curriculum and pedagogy contrive together to become complicit in their failure in early education and beyond. Until, children acquire a voice that is listened to and become more active participants in the cultures of their settings, whatever the nature of the curriculum, very little is likely to change.

Conclusion

Bernstein (1990) defines curriculum as the organization of knowledge and pedagogy as the transmission of knowledge; later refining this to include conduct, knowledge, practice and criteria (Bernstein 1996). Bruce (2006) defines pedagogy simply as the 'interface' between the child and the curriculum which you might think incorporates or rationalizes Bernstein's approach quite effectively in the context of this chapter. Whilst the curriculum might reflect a societal or governmental view on *what* knowledge should be transmitted, it is the pedagogy, the mode of that transmission and the relationship between the learner and the acquirer, that appears to have the greatest impact on learning. You will find that we revisit these ideas elsewhere in this book.

However, how practitioners construct that pedagogy may to some extent be defined by the nature of the curriculum itself. It would appear that in early years classrooms in the United Kingdom, whether we follow the National Curriculum or the Early Years Foundation Stage Framework there is still an emphasis on measurable learning outcomes represented by targets that children must reach by a given age. So, although the principles underpinning these frameworks may be different, the intrinsic values are much the same, in contrast to the early years provision of some other countries to whom you have been introduced in this chapter who have prioritized children's voice and visibility and thereby begun to comply with Article 12 of the UN Convention on the Rights of the Child.

The Early Years Foundation Stage is designed to be more than a curriculum framework focused on children's learning, and should perhaps always be viewed within a social policy context. Have a look at the final reflective activity:

Reflection

So . . . . The title of this chapter is Earlier and Earlier to School?

1. Does earlier and earlier curriculumization make any difference?
2. If the Early Years Foundation Stage is designed to bring together all aspects of a child's care and education from birth to five, why has a particular focus been put on educational settings, rather than, for example, the police, social services, NHS?

From what you have read in this chapter, you may consider that over time educational principles have completely given way to political expediency and that education, continually deluged over the past three decades with new educational initiatives, has borne the brunt of this. However, you may also recall that the Early Years Foundation Stage is underpinned by the outcomes of Every Child Matters, an agenda put into place in the wake of Lord Lamming's damning report into the death of Victoria Climbie, implicating not only education, but the police, social services and the NHS in its criticism. Why is it then that Government has increasingly reached towards education to exemplify their ideological position in what Hayes and Butterworth (2001) describe as the bureaucratic interventionist approach and which Richards (1999) calls 'democratic totalitarianism'? As suggested at the beginning of the chapter, education operates in a standards driven environment and it is this continual drive for schools to move forward and embrace everlasting swathes of new initiatives that leads to a 'climate of compliance' (Hayes and Butterworth 201), setting them apart from other agencies and allowing them to become easy fodder for constant Government intervention. Just as the child's voice and visibility is undermined and subsumed by policy and curricula we see the same happening to the adult in their setting. The title of the book asks whose childhood is it anyway – children's, adults or policymakers? From what we have seen in this chapter, curricula and the ideologies behind them lie very firmly in the domain of the policy makers.

Summary

- The past 40 years have seen a great shift in the level of central control of primary and early years education in this country: from the Plowden Report (1967) which advocated informal learning and thematic planning based on children's interests; through to greater governmental control with the introduction of the National Curriculum in 1988; and then for the early years, the non-statutory Curriculum Guidance for the Foundation Stage in 2000 followed by Birth to Three Matters in 2002 and the statutory Early Years Foundation Stage in 2008.
- The early years curricula have emphasized the contradictory aims of promoting learning through play and also planning, structure, expectations and assessment.
- Children in Key Stage 1 do not have the luxury of at least contradictory aims – a very formal curriculum takes precedence over play despite the fact that evidence from other countries suggests that beginning formal education before the age of 7 is ineffective in the long term.
- Other countries offer alternative models for reflection, including the examples of *Reggio-Emilia* and *Te-Whariki* which are significant in their belief in empowering children and recognizing children's rights.
- In this country, the problem and solutions may lie in the conceptualization and re-conceptualization of children and their place in society.

Recommended Reading

Cooper, H. and Sixsmith, C. (2008) *Teaching Across the Early Years 3-8: Curriculum Coherence and Continuity*. London: Routledge Falmer.

Dunlop, A. W. and Fabian, H. (2006) *Informing Transitions in the Early Years: Research, Policy and Practice*. London: Open University.

Hutchin, V. (2007) *Supporting Every Child's Learning Across the Early Years Foundation Stage*. London: Hodder Murray.

Nurse, A. D. (2007) *The New Early Years Professional: Dilemmas and Debates*. London: David Fulton.

Sylva, K., Sammons, P., Melhuish, E. C. and Siraj-Blatchford, I. (2001) *An Introduction to the Effective Provision of Pre-school Education (EPPE) Project* (The Effective Provision of Pre-school Education Project: Technical Paper). London: Institute of Education.

Bibliography

Abbott, L. and Rodger, R. (eds) (1994) *Quality Education in the Early Years*. Buckingham: Open University Press.

Barber, M. (2004) Paper given at Primary National Strategy Conference – audio transcript. [Online] Available at: http://www.ncsl.org.uk/media/F7B/90/primary-transcript-barber.pdf [Accessed 18 June 2008].

Bell, D. (2003) in Northen, S. (2003) Play. *Times Educational Supplement (TES)* [online] 2 May. Available at: http://tes.co.uk\section\story [Accessed 28 June 2008].

Bennett, N., Wood, E. and Rogers, S. (1997) *Teaching through Play: Teachers, Theories and Classroom Practice*. Buckingham: Open University Press.

Bernstein, B. (1990) *Class, Codes and Control, Vol. 4: The Structuring of Pedagogic Discourse*. London: Routledge.

Bernstein, B. (1996). *Pedagogy, Symbolic Control and Identity: Theory, Research, Critique*. London: Taylor and Francis.

Bertram, T. and Pascal, C. (2002) *Early Years Education: An International Perspective*. London: QCA [Online]. Available at: http://www.inca.org.uk/pdf/dearly_years.pdf. [Accessed 23 June 2008].

Bruce, T. (2001) *Learning through Play – Babies, Toddlers and the Foundation Years*. London: Hodder & Stoughton.

Bruce, T. (2005) (3rd edn) *Early Childhood Education*. Abingdon: Hodder Arnold.

Bruce, T. (2006) Plenary address at conference – 'After Rose – Which Way Forward'. Roehampton University, July 2006.

Central Advisory Council for Education (1967) *Children and Their Primary Schools* (The Plowden Report). London: HMSO.

Children's Workforce Development Council (CWDC) (2006) *Background to Pedagogues*. [Online]. Available at: http://www.cwdcouncil.org.uk/projects/pedagogues.htm [Accessed 30 June 2008].

Crook, D. and Aldrich, R. (eds) (2001) *History of Education for the Twenty-First Century*. London: Institute of Education.

David, T., Goouch, K., Powell, S. and Abbott, L. (2002) *A Review of the Literature to Support Birth to Three Matters* [Online]. Available at: http://www.surestart.gov.uk/_doc/0-99C16C.pdf [Accessed 24 June 2008].

DfEE/QCA (1999) National Curriculum Key Stages 1 and 2. London: DfEE/QCA.

DfEE/QCA (2000) *Curriculum Guidance for the Foundation Stage*. London: DfEE/QCA.

DfEE (2001) *The National Childcare Strategy* (Green Paper). London: DfES.

Department of Education and Science (DES) (1981) *The School Curriculum*. London: Department of Education and Science.

DfES (1990) *Starting with Quality: The Report of the Committee of Inquiry into the Quality of the Educational Experience Offered to 3 and 4 Year Olds. (The Rumbold Report)* London: HMSO.

DfES (2003) *Every Child Matters* (Green Paper) [Online]. Available at: http://www.dfes.gov.uk/consultations/downloadableDocs/EveryChildMatters.pdf [Accessed 26 June 2008].

DfES/Sure Start (2004a) *The Effective Provision of Pre-School Education (EPPE) Project: Final Report A Longitudinal Study Funded by the DfES* 1997–2004. London: DfES.

DfES/HM Treasury (2004b) *Choice for Parents, the Best Start for Children: A Ten Year Strategy for Childcare* [Online]. Available at: http://www.everychildmatters.gov.uk/_files/C7A546CB4579620B 7381308E1C161A9D.pdf [Accessed 26 June 2008].

DfES (2006) *Independent Review of the Teaching of Early Reading (Rose Review).* Nottingham: DfES.

DfES (2007) *Practice Guidance for the Early Years Foundation Stage.* Nottingham: DfES.

Edwards, C., Gandini, L. and Forman, G. (eds) (1993) *The Hundred Languages of Children: The Reggio Emilia Approach to Early Childhood Education.* Norwood, NJ: Ablex Publishing Corporation.

Featherstone, S. (2005) *Making it Work in Year 1.* Bosworth: Featherstone Educational Ltd.

Goldschmeid, E. and Jackson, S. (1994) *People Under Three: Young Children in Day Care.* London: Routledge.

Hammarberg, T. (2007) *Viewpoint – Listen Seriously to the Views of Children.* [Online] Available at: http://www.coe.int/t/commissioner/Viewpoints/071119_en.asp [Accessed 30 June 2008].

Hayes, D and Butterworth, S. (2001) Teacher activism in primary schools in England, *Teacher Development,* 5, 3.

Hepplewhite, D. (2005) *Times Educational Supplement (TES) Staffroom* [Online] 4 September. Available at: http://www8.tex.co.uk/section/staffroom/thread.aspx?story [Accessed 27 June 2008].

Hutt, S. J., Tyler, S., Hutt, C. and Christopherson, H. (1979) *Play, Learning and Exploration.* London: Routledge.

Independent Schools Council (2008) *Independent Schools and the Early Years Foundation Stage* [Online]. Available at www.isc.co.uk./eyfs [Accessed 6 May 2008].

Jowett, S. and Sylva, K. (1986) Does kind of pre-school matter? *Educational Research,* 28, 1, 21.

Katz, L. and Chard, S. (2000) (2nd edn) *Engaging Children's Minds – The Project Approach.* New York: Ablex.

Ministry of Education, New Zealand (1996) *Te Whariki/Early Childhood Curriculum.* Wellington, NZ: Learning Media. [Online]. Available at http://www.minedu.govt.nz/web/downloadable/dl3567_ v1/whariki.pdf [Accessed 24 June 2008].

Moyles, J. (2005) (2nd edn) *The Excellence of Play.* Buckingham: Open University Press.

National Society for the Prevention of Cruelty to Children (2006) The NSPCC response to the Early Years Foundation Stage framework (Department for Education and Skills) [Online] Available at www.nspcc.org.uk/public affairs [Accessed 20 May 2008].

Nutbrown, C. (2000) With due respect: 'making sure' for childhoods in the 21st century, in *The Future for Childhood. Alliance for Childhood Articles for the Brussels Conference 2000.* [Online]. Available at http://www.allianceforchildhood.org.uk/index.php?id=34 [Accessed 2 June 2008].

OfSTED (2003) *The Education of Six Year Olds in England, Denmark and Finland – An International Comparative Study.* Available at: http://www.ofsted.gov.uk/publications/index.cfm?fuseaction= pubs.displayfile&id=3327&type=pdf [Accessed 9 June 2008].

OfSTED (2004) *Transition from the Reception Year to Year 1.* London: OfSTED.

Pollard, A. (2002) *Reflective Teaching in the Primary School.* Abingdon: Hodder Arnold.

Qualifications and Curriculum Authority/Primary National Strategy (2005) *Continuing the Learning Journey* (training package). Norwich: QCA.

QCA, 2008. A big picture of the Curriculum, [Online]. Available at http://www.qca.org.uk/library Assets/media/Big_Picture_2008.pdf [Accessed 10 June 2008].

Richards, C. (1999) *Primary Education: At a Hinge of History*. London: Falmer.

Riley, J. (ed). (2003) *Learning in the Early Years. A Guide for Teachers of Children 3–7*. London: Paul Chapman Publishing.

Robinson, K. and Jones-Diaz, C. (2006) *Diversity and Difference in Early Childhood Education*. London: McGraw Hill.

Sanders, D., White, G., Burge, B., Sharp, C., Eames, A., McEnue, R and Grayson, H. (2005) *A Study of the Transition from the Foundation Stage to Key Stage 1* (DfES Research Report SSU/2005/FR/013). London: DfES.

School Curriculum and Assessment Authority (SCAA) (1996) *Desirable Learning Outcomes*. London: SCAA.

Schweinhart, L. J., Weikart, D. P. and Larner, M. B. (1986). Consequences of three preschool curriculum models through age 15, *Early Childhood Research Quarterly*, 1, 15–45. Cited in: Slavin, R. E., Karweit, N. L. and Madden, N. A. (1989). *Effective Programs for Students at Risk*. Needham Heights, MA: Allyn and Bacon.

Soler, J. and Miller, L. (2003) The struggle for early childhood curricula: a comparison of the English Foundation Stage Curriculum, *Te Whāriki* and *Reggio Emilia*, *International Journal of Early Years Education*, 11, 1, March 2003, 57–68 (12). London: Routledge.

Staggs, L. (2005) cited in Featherstone, S. (2005) *Making it Work in Year 1*. Bosworth: Featherstone Education Ltd.

Sure Start (2002) *Birth to 3 Matters: A Framework to Support Children in Their Earliest Years*. Nottingham: DCSF Publications.

UK Parliament (1988) The Education Reform Act. [Online] Available at http://www.opsi.gov.uk/acts/ acts1988/ukpga_19880040_en_1 [Accessed 19 June 2008].

UK Parliament (2001) Select Committee on Education and Employment First Report [Online]. Available from: http://www.publications.parliament.uk/pa/cm200001/cmselect/cmeduemp/33/ 3306.htm [Accessed 18 June 2008].

United Nations (1989) Convention on the Rights of the Child. [Online]. Available from: http://www. unhchr.ch/html/menu3/b/k2crc.htm [Accessed 3 June 2008].

Waters, M. (2008) Director of Curriculum, QCA. *A Curriculum for the 21st Century* [Online]. Available from: http://www.nga.org.uk/uploads/QCA%20Supplement.pdf [Accessed 18 June 2008].

West, A. and Varlaam, A. (1990). Does it matter when children start school?, *Educational Research*, 32, 3, 210–217.

Wood, E. (2007) Reconceptualising Child-Centred Education: contemporary directions in policy, theory and practice in early childhood, *FORUM: for promoting 3–19 comprehensive education*, 49, 1, 119–134. Oxford: Symposium Journals.

4

Integrating Professional Roles in Early Years around Children's Lives and Learning

Jane Tarr

Introduction

The main argument outlined in this chapter will provide fresh insight into developing policy related to young children's care and education. It is noted that the roles of practitioners in the early years sector of the children's workforce are being reconceptualized through a range of policy directives that include new sets of competencies and standards for those working in maintained and non-maintained sectors. The particular issue explored in this chapter is the extent to which these new policy drives recognize a core duty of professionals working with young children – the duty to facilitate children's awareness of their rights and their responsibilities. Such awareness will enable children to claim their childhood and become effective participators. Thus the main argument explores the extent to which practitioners working with young children see their various roles as being integrated around this central purpose.

Key Questions

- What policy initiatives encourage professionals to build young children's capacity to realize their rights and responsibilities?
- What distinctive roles do different professionals play in relation to young children?
- How integrated is professional work with young children and their families?
- To what extent does a framework of key rights and responsibilities support us in answering the question, whose childhood is it?
- How might professionals working with young children develop further their roles in relation to children's participation?

Building children's capacity for independence

In the United Kingdom the demand for high quality care and education for children from birth to five has grown and government response has been to reconceptualize provision with the creation of new contexts (Sure Start Children's Centres 1999), new professional roles (Early Years Professional Status 2006) and new standards for learning, development and care (Early Years Foundation Curriculum 2008). Analysis of these initiatives, created by Ball and Vincent (2005) has sought to understand the driving purpose behind such provision asking such questions:

> Is such a policy designed to enhance the quality of experience for young children through developing the parenting skills of new families? Is it to raise the educational standards of young children? Is it to bring communities of young children and their families together for greater social inclusion and cohesion across diverse groups? Is it to ensure that young children are raised out of poverty by providing childcare and enabling their parents to work?

We could add to these by asking if children are enabled to take responsibility for themselves within such developments?

The purpose behind the Sure Start initiative, at the start of the early years reform process, combines all these goals in a statement:

> It is the cornerstone of the Government's drive to tackle child poverty and social exclusion working with parents-to-be, parents/carers and children to promote the physical, intellectual and social development of babies and young children so that they can flourish at home and when they get to school. (Sure Start 1999)

The one aspect that appears not to be included is the consultation with children themselves on the reform process. Whilst development of provision will impact upon the experience of young children, little research has taken place to collect children's views about these developments. A paper forming part of the primary review looked at research concerning children's views on their primary schools and concluded that it was necessary to develop a *'more appropriate understanding of children as social actors within their cultures and communities, and of how education fits into and contributes to their lives as a whole'* (Robinson and Fielding 2007, p. 20). It is hard to find any mention of young children's views about their education and care. The Sure Start website does not include mention of the participation of young children or to building young children's understanding of their rights and their responsibilities. The absence of such evidence communicates negatively about the relationships between adults and young children in the United Kingdom and does not support the rhetoric of participation that can be found in some documentation, for example, 'Working Together: listening to the voices of children and young people' (DCSF 2008c).

The vision for children in society as stated by the New Labour government relies heavily on the availability and quality of early childhood education and care to ensure the new generation have the best start in life – quality experiences in their daycare provision, educational opportunities at an early stage, capacity to socialize with others and be free from poverty with both parents able to work. This is consistently stated in documentation and clearly articulated in the DfES Ten Year Strategy for Childcare:

> Government has long recognized the collective interest in ensuring that children get a good start in life: it is in the nation's social and economic interests: children are citizens, workers, parents and leaders of the future. It is in everyone's interests that children are given the opportunity to fulfill their potential… Investment in children to ensure they have opportunities and capabilities to contribute in positive ways throughout their lives is money well spent and it will reduce the cost of social failure. (DfES 2004, 2.11)

One can begin to see the expectations of the United Nations Convention on the Rights of the Child (UNCRC 1989) reflected in the language of this document, yet the UK Children's Commissioners report (June 2008) still states that *The UNCRC has not been fully brought into legislative and policy processes in England* (UK Commissioners Report 2008, p. 5). The challenge to bring about change within professional practice requires more direct statements and specific inclusion within sets of competencies and standards to empower professionals to develop integrated working practice centred on the rights and responsibilities of young children. Such a focus can unite the wide range of professionals working in children's services in a common goal to ensure that *'Children and young people will have far more say about issues that affect them as individuals and collectively'* *(Every Child Matters (2003)*. The range of professionals involved in working with young children have distinctive contributions to make but one overall goal that brings them together is an overarching duty to be responsive to the expressed concerns of their clients through promoting direct and responsible participation of all young children and their families.

Much of government policy within early years encourages professionals to work closely with the community, with parents, with other professionals and to listen to and respect young children (e.g. Practice Guidance for the Early Years Foundation Stage 2008b). Such integrated working practice has the potential to build greater collective understanding of childhood. If all adults are responding to the behaviours of young children and sharing their insights with relevant professionals in collaborative dialogic exchanges then early years provision is vibrant, dynamic and relevant to children's requirements. In a review of provision for young children and the relevant staff training across Europe conducted in the late 1990s it was recognized that

> Institutional childcare in developmentally appropriate surroundings is regarded not only as an educational and social opportunity for children but also as a forum for parent participation and community orientation. (Oberhuemer and Ulich 1997, p. 8)

Integrated working practice involves all professionals engaging with the local communities they serve and parents and carers with and for young children. This is the central focus of their work whether they are generic early years workers or whether they have specific contributions to make in the education, care or health of young children.

The state involvement in what happens during the education and care of young children has extended now to start from birth. There is debate as to whether such state intervention is beneficial, but practitioners appear to welcome the Early Years Foundation Stage framework as it provides recognition of their work and acknowledges the integral links between learning, development and care (EYFS 2008). It is interesting to note the recent emphasis being placed in the secondary school curriculum within a framework for personal learning and thinking skills. Here young people are empowered to become *independent enquirers, creative thinkers, reflective learners, team workers, self managers and effective participators* (QCA 2008). These sets of skills reflect the aims of the UNCRC and would ensure that young people do realize their rights and their responsibilities. Such a set of skills can also be found for young children in early years settings in the EYFS section on 'personal, social and emotional development'. Here all professionals, generic early years professionals or health visitors or social workers are encouraged to focus on the following aspects of personal development: *dispositions and attitudes, self-confidence and self-esteem, making relationships, behaviour and self control, self-care and sense of community* (EYFS Practice Guidance 2008, p. 26–41).

Further reading

Read the UN Convention on the Rights of the Child Part 1 (http://www2.ohchr.org/english/law/crc.htm) and identify any Articles which you think closely relate to the following documents:

The group of skills expressed in the QCA document *Framework For Personal Learning And Thinking Skills* for secondary-aged pupils (QCA 2008) and

The Early Years Foundation Stage Practice Guidance, section on Personal, social and emotional development pages 26–41 (DCSF 2008b)

The Early Years Foundation Stage became mandatory in September 2008 for all early years providers attended by young children *'from birth to the end of the academic year in which a child has their fifth birthday'* and for such providers to register with OfSTED, including schools with children of such an age in reception classes. The non-statutory practice guidance for meeting the requirements of the EYFS are intended to guide the work of all early years' practitioners regardless of their distinctive training, discipline, or background. The framework has a strong emphasis on learning and development which are the concerns of all professionals working in children's services – whether they are from the voluntary sector, the local community, are qualified teachers or learning support assistants with an educational background, come with welfare and social care perspectives on young children or are medical and health practitioners. Such a framework has the potential to support further integrated working practice amongst early year's practitioners.

Early years' practitioners, professional roles and responsibilities

Across Europe it is understood that more structured care and educational provision outside the home is required for young children (birth to 5/7 years). The demand within the United Kingdom has primarily been met by the private and voluntary sector which would include extended family members, informal child minders, local playgroups and private day nurseries. The new Labour government has been committed to ensuring high quality facilities for children in their early years and has embarked upon a series of major initiatives to ensure that such providers have the required knowledge and skills. The Effective Provision of Pre-School Education Project (EPPE) (Sylva et al. 2004) found that early years settings where staff have higher qualifications, have a marked impact on the quality of provision offered, resulting in improved outcomes for young children.

The Children's Workforce Development Council (CWDC) was set up in 2005 to support the implementation of the Every Child Matters programme and exists to improve the lives of children, by ensuring that the people working with them have the best possible training and advice. The occupational roles they seek to support that fall within the early years sector cover: early years workers in playgroups, children's centres, day nurseries, nursery schools and nursery classes in primary schools; registered child minders , nannies, Portage workers, foster carers, children and families social workers, family centre workers, outreach or family support workers, and anyone who works with children and young people in the voluntary sector, including volunteers, who are not covered by another sector skills body. Many of the roles and responsibilities have not been fully recognized in the past and are now receiving attention and scrutiny from the government. As such there are mixed responses from the early years sector but on the whole workers are welcoming opportunities to engage in recognition of their expertise. The CWDC provides a very helpful outline of some of these roles together with qualification requirements, rates of pay and other useful information CWDC (2008).

The remit of CWDC however does not cover all professional groups who work with young children. Examples are teachers or health visitors who have their own professional bodies such as the Training and Development Agency for Schools (TDA) or Skills for Health. In order to encourage a greater understanding of services that are specifically focused on children and young people, such professionals are drawn together through the Children's Workforce Network. The Children's Workforce Network (CWN) was set up as a voluntary alliance to bring together relevant Sector Skills Councils, including the Children's Workforce Development Council and other partners such as Nursing and Midwifery Council, General Social Care Council, TDA, General Teaching Council and the National College for School Leadership. The alliance produces a helpful e-bulletin bi-monthly that provides updates on policy and practice across the children and young people's workforce (Children's Workforce Network 2008b).

Early years practitioners have historically been undervalued which is reflected in levels of pay and levels of qualifications for the work. New Labour strategy to alter this is to be welcomed. The opportunities it represents are illuminating, particularly because of the recognition afforded to workers' knowledge and skills through a process of assessment and professional development. Tricia David calls for training that is not simply about acquiring facts and knowledge but about '*exploring bodies of knowledge and submitting them to critical analysis in the light of real-life experience*' with opportunities for '*depersonalised self-evaluation of strengths and weaknesses*' (David in Abbott and Pugh 1998, p. 25). Such an approach is now more accessible through study on early years foundation degrees, designed with employers to acknowledge and respect practitioners work-based experience and learning. The assessment only route to gaining Early Years Professional Status (EYPS 2006) is another example of how the education system is able to recognize the knowledge and skills held by previously unqualified early years workers. However one of the greatest challenges for this process of training and accreditation is for some practitioners to reconceptualize away from an understanding of young children as '*human becomings*' or '*citizens in waiting*' and to acknowledge that very young children are trying hard to participate and make sense of their worlds and need adults to provide quite specific support and encouragement.

The CWDC has a participation strategy for their own organization, to include children, young people, their parents and families and states that it '*adopts the UN Convention on the Rights of the Child*'. It has produced a poster of the UNCRC in child-friendly language for children and those working with them to download. More recently this aspect of their work has been re-emphasized with the appointment of a Participation Coordinator and 12 participation champions whose work is to embed the policy of participation across the whole organization. Their working definition is that *'participation means ensuring the structures, resources and processes are in place so we and our workforce can take action, make changes and be steered by what children, young people and their families tell us'* (CWN e-bulletin no. 9 February/March 2008, p. 7) The outcomes of this development are not yet reported on the CWDC website but one hopes that such an investment will have an impact on the professional roles supported by CWDC and subsequently on the experience of young children.

Wider workforce for all children in the early years

The expansion of the early years sector is taking place alongside the call through the Every Child Matters Agenda, for all professionals working in children's services to operate in a more integrated 'joined-up' manner to meet the needs of the more vulnerable children and families. There are many professionals across children's services whose expertise and distinctive contribution may be required to support young children and their families. These might include local community members to provide background knowledge and insight; educational psychologists to assess and advise practitioners with concerns about a child's development; curriculum advisers to support practitioners in differentiating the stated areas of learning and development for young children with difficulties arising from physical, sensory or communicative difficulties; health practitioners to set up intervention programmes designed to enhance healthy development or social workers to enable workers in early years settings to understand the challenges of a child's specific home context.

Children's Centres and extended schools are being developed to enable professionals working in children's services to work in a closer, more integrated way for children and their families. The locational aspect of this within children's centres or extended schools is essential for those children with additional support requirements and their families who may need to access a wide range of other professionals. The following case study of Julie provides a stimulus for considering the value and benefit of integrated working for Julie and her family.

Case Study: Julie

Julie is three years old and was diagnosed at birth with cerebral palsy. She has weekly visits at home from the physiotherapist and also is expected to visit the hospital regularly to see the paediatrician responsible for her development. The family have contact with an occupational therapist who advises on different kinds of equipment and resources that might help Julie in her mobility. At one stage she was seeing the audiologist as there have been concerns about her hearing and she is currently undergoing extensive tests to ascertain the level of her vision which we expect will require her to wear glasses. Julie is a calm, friendly little girl with two younger siblings.

1. How might a local children's centre support Julie and her family?
2. What kind of support do you think they require and from whom?
3. To what extent can this process invite participation and promote responsibility for both Julie and her family?

The Special Educational Needs Code of Practice (2001) includes a full section (DfES 2001, p. 27–31) on how to ensure the participation of the child in decision making about their educational and social provision. It is one of the few documents of its time that cites the UNCRC (1989) whilst recognizing the challenge of accessing the voice of a child with disabilities.

> Ascertaining the child's views may not always be easy. Very young children and those with severe communication difficulties, for example, may present a significant challenge for education, health and other professionals. But the principle of seeking and taking account of the ascertainable views of the child or young person is an important one. Their perceptions and experiences can be invaluable to professionals in reaching decisions. LEAs, schools and early education settings should make arrangements to enable this to happen. (DfES 2001 p. 27)

It may be that professionals working with more vulnerable children have had to face the challenge earlier but it is interesting that such professionals have recognized the value and benefit of children's participation and are rising to the challenge (Cavet and Sloper 2004). The Common Assessment Framework (CAF) is another tool which is designed to bring different professionals to work together. This document may eventually replace the statementing procedure and enable all relevant professionals to contribute to an overall assessment of need for a child who has any additional support requirements in order to access education or care within children's services. There are a wide range of training resources supporting the use of the CAF available on the ECM website (see www.everychildmatters.gov.uk).

The CWN has adopted a set of values for integrated working with children and young people that support all practitioners in this challenging work. The statement of values builds upon the fact that all practitioners recognize and uphold children's rights as expressed in the UNCRC.

> Practitioners are committed to engaging children, young people and families fully in identifying goals, assessing options, making decisions and reviewing outcomes. They support children's and families' involvement in issues that matter to them, including through involvement in the development and evaluation of children's services. (Children's Workforce Network 2008)

This statement has been shared with training providers in the education field by the TDA as part of a consultation about a foundation degree framework for the school workforce. The early years sector has a reputation for ensuring a high level of inter professional working practice as it is realized that early recognition of difficulties can lead to better outcomes for children. Sharing insights across different disciplines is essential for early years practitioners who are required to hold a holistic understanding of the child with understanding of educational, health, social, environmental and cognitive aspects to the child as evidenced in the four themes below designed to guide their work:

> A Unique Child – every child is a competent learner from birth who can be resilient, capable, confident and self-assured.
> Positive Relationships – children learn to be strong and independent from a base of loving and secure relationships with parents and/or a key person.
> Enabling Environments – the environment plays a key role in supporting and extending children's development and learning.
> Learning and Development – children develop and learn in different ways and at different rates and all areas of Learning and Development are equally important and inter-connected. (EYFS 2008, p. 05)

All professionals working in early years settings, whatever their discipline or background, were required from September 2008 to recognize their role and responsibilities within the EYFS (2008). The expansion and professionalizing of the children's workforce will, it is hoped, lead to more adults being aware of young children's own expressions of their needs and be able to facilitate their capacity to address difficulties in a responsible way. It is important that all early years practitioners and professionals from across children's services working with very young children, remain vigilant at this time to the responses and behaviours of young children for whom these developments are intended. It is their childhood, their opinions matter and need to be taken seriously. The common 'integrating' duty for all professionals is to ensure an enhanced early years provision that encourages young children to be self assured, confident, capable, resilient, responsible and effective today as well as for their futures.

Emerging rationale for underpinning professional roles within the UNCRC

One of the key documents for the training and professional development of the children's workforce has been The Common Core Skills and Knowledge for the Children's Workforce (DfES 2005). The content of this document has been embedded into the standards for Qualified Teacher Status; it is an integral part of training to be a social worker and has been adapted into a checklist for all health and medical practitioners who are working with children and young people. It provides a comprehensive outline of the knowledge and skills necessary for anyone working with children and young people. It is divided into six sections:

1. Effective communication and engagement with children, young people, their families and carers
2. Child and young person development
3. Safeguarding and promoting the welfare of the child
4. Supporting transitions
5. Multi-agency working
6. Sharing information (DfES 2005)

Whilst this document explicitly states that it acknowledges the rights of children and young people, and the role parents, carers and families play in helping children and young people achieve the outcomes identified in Every Child Matters (DfES 2005: 4), it contains absolutely no further encouragement to practitioners working with children and young people to develop their clients' capacity to understand their rights and responsibilities. A brief mention appears in the section concerned with safeguarding children stating that practitioners should have the confidence to represent actively the child or young person and his or her rights (Common Core, DfES 2005, p. 14). This limited recognition of the rights and responsibilities of children has resulted in continued criticism from the Joint Committee on Human Rights reporting in 2003: 'We regret that the Government has abandoned its commitment to publish an over-arching strategy for children with the UNCRC as its framework (House of Lords and House of Commons 2003). They sought child-impact assessment approaches which have still not yet been devised. Whilst the rhetoric of Every Child Matters (2003) places the child at the centre of change, the centrality of children's voices and viewpoints is minimized. Initially the voluntary sector was engaged to consult with children and young people preceding the Every Child Matters publication. Child-friendly reports were produced and many children and young people became engaged in the debate. One of the main issues raised by children and young people was their need to have 'safe places to play' which led to some local authorities developing play strategies. Some five years on the UK Commissioners' Report to the UN Committee on the Rights of the Child (2008) has the following recommendations which are directly relevant to very young children:

Recommendations

R87 The UK Government and devolved administrations must take further steps to address the barriers to children's right to play.

R88 The UK Government and devolved administrations must urgently address the widely held intolerance of children in public spaces.

R89 The UK Government and devolved administrations should ensure fully inclusive play provision for children with disabilities.

R90 The UK Government and devolved administrations should address the reduction in play spaces for children and ensure that the views of children are listened to in planning decisions. There should be a statutory duty on local authorities to make adequate free provision for children's play up to age 18.

UK Commissioners' Report to the UN Committee on the Rights of the Child (2008, p. 29)

These arguments are not new. Indeed national policy under the overall agenda of Every Child Matters presented the outcomes for children as imperatives in the initial documentation (ECM 2003, p. 25), inciting them to take responsibility for their lives and for public services to support them in this process. The stated imperatives for children demonstrate the governments' willingness to consult children, 'Be healthy, Stay safe, Enjoy and achieve, Make a positive contribution and Achieve economic well-being' (Every Child Matters, DfES 2003, p. 25). In this way the integrating duty of all workers in early years settings is clarified. There is a common and accepted requirement to demonstrate their capacity to understand the views and wishes of young children. According to the government report to the UNCRC in 2007,

> Research carried out with children and young people in England found that just under half (44%) of children and young people felt that they were not given enough respect and understanding by adults. Whilst youth workers and community development workers were perceived as giving the most respect, politicians and teachers were perceived as giving the least. The research also found that children of all ages wanted to be informed and involved in decision making concerning their families, education, care and politics. (DCSF 2007, p. 41)

This research did not include very young children for whom the challenge is greatest. The mosaic approach proposed in 2001 comprises of a multi-method approach to listening to young children in order that their views might inform the reform of children's services (Clark and Moss 2001). Their approach to gain insight into young children's perspectives, was a combination of talking and observing children together with their own photographs, pictures and maps and representing these for others to understand. You will find examples of this approach elsewhere in this book.

Indeed in the early years of life, children are highly dependent upon adults for care and protection, but the institutions of the twenty-first century need to enable very young children to become independent, self reliant, confident and responsible in order to meet the five outcomes stated in ECM (2003), encouraged by all members of the children's workforce. The government is continuing to 'up-skill and professionalise' the early years workforce with a particular focus on the private and voluntary sector where they consider the standards are most variable (Building Brighter Futures, DCSF 2008a). The new professional contexts, new professional roles and new frameworks for learning and development have the potential to draw adults together around families with young children to enhance everyone's understanding of young children. If all professionals enable young children to understand their rights and their responsibilities as individuals and as a collective then we can maintain high quality and relevant early years provision that is child centred. We can give childhood back to the children.

Summary

- There are a wide range of professionals working with children in their early years including those with a broad generic understanding of young children and experts from education, social care and health backgrounds. All are valuable for young children and their families
- This wide range of professionals and para-professionals need to work together in an integrated manner to ensure the highest quality of service for young children and their families
- All professions focus on the quality of the child's experience and require additional training to enable them to facilitate children's understanding of their rights and responsibilities based on the UNCRC
- Children need to be respected and listened to in all matters that affect them and facilitated to participate in ways that enhance their own lives and learning.

Recommended Reading

Clark, A. (2005) *Beyond Listening: Children's Perspectives on Early Childhood Services*. London: Policy Press.

Ball, M. O. G. (2003) *School Inclusion: The School, the Family and the Community.* York: Joseph Rowntree Foundation.

Anning A., Cottrell D., Frost N., Green J. and Robinson M. (2006) *Developing Multi-Professional Teamwork for Integrated Children's Services*. Maidenhead: Open University Press.

Bibliography

Abbott, L. and Pugh, G. (1998) *Training to Work in the Early Years: Developing the Climbing Frame.* Buckingham: Open University Press.

Ball, S. J. and Vincent, C. (2005) The 'childcare champion'? New Labour, social justice and the childcare market, *British Educational Research Journal*, 31, 5, 557–570.

Cavet, J. and Sloper, P. (2004) Participation of disabled children in individual decisions about their lives and in public decisions about service development, *Children & Society*, 18, 278–290.

Clark, A. (2005) *Beyond Listening: Children's Perspectives on Early Childhood Services*. London: Policy Press.

Clark, A. and Moss, P. (2001) *Listening to Young Children: The Mosaic Approach*. London: National Children's Bureau Enterprises.

Children's Workforce Network (CWN) (2008a) e-bulletin no. 09 February/March 2008 http://www.childrensworkforce.org.uk/?lid=271 [Accessed 27 July 2008].

Children's Workforce Network (CWN) (2008b) Values for integrated working with children and young people www.childrensworkforce.org.uk [Accessed 15 July 2008].

CWDC (2006) Early Years Professional Status.

CWDC (2008) (http://www.cwdcouncil.org.uk/workforce-data/occupational-summaries [Accessed 23 July 2008].

Department of Education and Skills (DfES) (2001) *Special Educational Needs Code of Practice*. Nottingham: DfES Publications.

Department of Education and Skills (DfES) (2003) *Every Child Matters*. London: Stationary Office.

Department of Education and Skills (DfES) (2004) *Choice for Parents, the Best Start for Children: A Ten Year Childcare Strategy*. London: Stationary Office.

DfES (2005) *The Common Core Skills and Knowledge for the Children's Workforce*. London: DCSF.

DCSF (2007) *The Early Years Foundation Stage*. London: DCSF.

DCSF (2008a) *Building Brighter Futures: Next Steps for the Children's Workforce*. Nottingham: DCSF Publications.

DCSF (2008b) Practice Guidance for the Early Years Foundation Stage 2008 (http://www.standards.dfes.gov.uk/eyfs/resources/downloads/practice-guidance.pdf) [Accessed 20 November 2008].

DCSF (2008c) *Working Together: Listening to the Voices of Children and Young People*. Nottingham: DCSF Publications.

Every Child Matters (2004) (http://www.everychildmatters.gov.uk/aims [Accessed 12 June 2008].

Glass, N. (1999) Sure Start: the development of an early intervention programme for young children, in the *United Kingdom Children and Society*, 13, 257–264.

House of Lords and House of Commons (2003) The Government's Response to the Committee's Tenth Report of Session 2002–03 on the UN Convention on the Rights of the Child http://www.publications.parliament.uk/pa/jt200203/jtselect/jtrights/187/187.pdf [Accessed 27 November 2008].

Jenks, C. (ed.) (1982) *The Sociology of Childhood: Essential Readings*. London: Batsford.

National Day Nurseries Association (NDNA) (2004) *Promoting Quality in the Early Years* Brighouse: NDNA.

Nurse, A. (ed.) (2007) *The New Early Years Professional: Dilemmas and Debates*. London: Routledge.

Oberhuemer, P. and Ulich, M. (1997) *Working with Young Children in Europe: Provision and Staff Training*. Paul Chapman Publishing.

Qualifications and Curriculum Authority (QCA) (2000) *Curriculum Guidance for the Foundation Stage*. London: Stationery Office.

Qualifications and Curriculum Authority (QCA) (2003) *Birth to Three Matters*. London: Stationery Office.

Qualifications and Curriculumn Authority (QCA) (2008) Framework for Personal Learning and Thinking Skills. http://www.qca.org.uk/libraryAssets/media/PLTS_framework.pdf [Accessed 19 February 2009].

Robinson, C. and Fielding, M. (2007) Research Survey 5/3: Children and their Primary Schools: Pupils' voices (www.primaryreview.org.uk) [Accessed 21 July 2008].

Siraj-Blatchford, I., Clarke, K. and Needham, M. (eds) (2007) *The Team around the Child: Multi Agency Working in the Early Years*. Stoke on Trent: Trentham Books.

Sure Start (1999) www.surestart.gov.uk [Accessed 20 July 2008].

Sylva, K., Melhuish, E., Sammons, P., Siraj-Blatchford, I. and Taggart, B. (2004) *The Effective Provision of Pre-School Education Project (EPPE): Findings from Pre-School to the End of Key Stage 1*. Nottingham: DfES.

UK Children's Commissioners' Report to UN Committee on the Rights of the Child (June 2008) www.childcom.org.uk/publications [Accessed 25 July 2008].

UNCRC (1989) www.unicef.org.uk [Accessed 20 July 2008].

Useful websites

www.unicef.org.uk

www.surestart.gov.uk

www.everychildmatters.gov.uk

www.qca.org.uk

www.cwdcouncil.org.uk

www.childrensworkforce.org.uk

www.childcom.org.uk

Part II
REPRESENTATION AND CHILDHOOD

Introduction

This section is best thought of as an exploration of a really big theme through four different areas of children's experience. Our big theme is representation, by this we mean making and taking meaning through contemporary media, talking, drawing, painting and playing.

In Chapter 5 Mandy Lee and Richard Eke discuss how children engage with a range of screens they become familiar with early in their lives. They argue that materials for young children present a limited voice for them and view of them. Although portrayals of children are becoming less stereotyped they argue that much work remains to be done. They suggest that young children are competent with a large range of technologies and deserve a respectful and committed media education.

In Chapter 6 John Lee and Richard Eke write about children's talk, moving from discussion of language acquisition and talk in domestic settings, to the increasingly formalized language of early years settings. They recognize the opportunities for proper conversations through shared sustained thinking and chart the decline of opportunities for such talk.

In Chapter 7 Richard Eke and John Lee turn their attention to further aspects of children's representational activity focusing on their graphic mark making. Again they place children's meanings as pivotal for such activity and are critical of the reductionist account of mark making in the practical guidance for the Early Years Foundation Stage.

In the concluding chapter, Chapter 8, Alison Bailey and Steve Barnes begin with a recognition of the importance of space to play for the development of children's wellbeing. They also acknowledge the detrimental consequences of the absence of such spaces. Steve and Alison discuss the places designed for children and the spaces children actually occupy. As well as recognizing spaces that seem to segregate children they also recognize the uniqueness of spaces that children find playable. Embedded in their argument is an assertion that if we consult with children we will create better spaces for everybody.

5

Children and Screens

Mandy Lee and Richard Eke

Chapter Outline

In this chapter we will introduce you to a critical approach to a variety of debates around how children engage with a range of screens that they become familiar with early in their lives. We think this is important because we believe cultural representations both reflect and shape children's experiences of the world. We want to talk about relationships between different media provided for children (TV, film, computers) and the way adults use these to construct representations of and for children and the sorts of sense children make of these.

We will start by exploring how young children read contemporary media representations and how they learn to become viewers and users of computers. We will look at what they do as individual meaning-makers as well as the social nature of meaning-making. We raise issues around how they make sense of what is on screen and the credence that they give to what they see.

We will then talk about how young children are represented, particularly on television and film and on computer games and online activities. Young children are defined as a distinct audience. Exploring the provision for this audience gives us an opportunity to see how this audience is constructed and we will recognize that this is not the only place where early childhood is constructed.

Key Questions

1. How do young children read the screen?
2. What ways of being for young children do adults create in contemporary media?
3. What are the consequences for the young child viewer and the adults around them?

How do young children read the screen?

The ways in which young children come to understand screens has been explored since the 1950s (Heuyer 1956) with observational studies of children's faces in the cinema, through a range of studies, especially American, of young children's television viewing, through to more recent studies of their engagement with computer screens. There has been a gradual shift from a focus on treating children's relationships with the screens they use as a matter for empirical investigation towards problematizing this relationship. In many respects this shift has paralleled moves towards presenting ideas of childhood as contested concepts (e.g. Prout 2000). Early researchers worked from an implicit model of the young viewer trapped in isolation with the screen (Anderson and Levin 1976). Later studies made use of an adult interlocutor (Collins et al. 1981) or were of an ethnographic nature (e.g. Australian, Palmer 1986, United Kingdom, Browne 1999) or were studies of the domestic experience of young children that included viewing (Walkerdine 1986). They indicated that isolated experience is unusual, with viewing often being part of playing at home and sometimes socially controlled by older siblings or by adults. As well as wanting to know how children become viewers making sense of what goes on the screen, there has also been a consistent interest in the consequences, either positive or negative, of using a screen.

Children do not usually become screen users in isolation but there are some personal achievements necessary to become users. Many of the characteristics of becoming a viewer were established by American researchers working with educational television and their work does focus on children as lone individuals watching the screen. Anderson and Lorch (1983) and their co-workers suggest that there is strong evidence that children first learn to attend to the screen when they are around two and half years old. Even so, much younger children are sensitive to audio-visual materials, indeed there is evidence that children as young as four months are capable of attending, and attend for longer to synchronized audio-visual presentations. Cognitively orientated researchers have consistently emphasized the meanings that children make and their debate largely settled on the importance of television formats and children's knowledge and understanding of the world. In exploring these dimensions the range of variables to be taken into account has been consistently expanded so that they include aspects of child identity (race, class and so on) and of the viewing context (adult interlocutor, small group) as well as specifically televisual features.

What these studies do tell us is that young viewers demonstrate through selective attention to the screen that they are making active viewing choices. Jaglom and Gardner (1981) conclude that by about two years of age children like to name characters, describing them in terms of a single characteristic and production location. Three to four year olds shift to identifying differences and similarities between characters and are able to discuss several features of them simultaneously, although the use of a single trait continues. By 5, children's systems of organization:

> [I]nclude individual shows as well as groups of show types classified in terms of visual format, target audience, scheduling, and purpose. Their system also includes individual characters who are linked primarily to individual shows, as well as character types that are grouped according to physical appearance, behavior, psychological characteristics and their interactions with others. (Jaglom and Gardner 1981, p. 22)

The work of Gibbon et al. (1986) suggested that children apply their knowledge and understanding of the world to the interpretation of televisual events; included in this understanding is one of how story structures work. Stein and Glenn (1979) showed the difference this knowledge made to the retellings of pre-school and first graders compared to those of third graders. Browne (1999) has argued that viewing experience may have the capacity to enhance younger children's understanding of story structures. A key concept in grappling with children's understanding of television has been the importance attached to attending to the screen and continuing to attend to it. If children are to understand what is going on they need to look at the screen and keep looking and so how to elicit and maintain a child's gaze has been a key feature of academic research.

Reflection

That is, the longer a young child has been looking at the screen, the longer he or she will continue to look; conversely, the longer the child has been sitting in front of the television but ignoring the screen, the less likely they are to start looking.

Liebert and Sprafkin (1988, p. 225)

- Can you think of routine social events that would disrupt a sustained look?
- Is there anything that you think might engage a child in looking at the screen?
- Can you categorize your responses in terms of the child as an individual, the child as a social person and the nature of the screen event?

The work of Anderson and Levin (1976) is especially important here and of particular interest since they worked with 1 to 4 year olds. Their most consistent finding was that action played a major role in holding children's attention. Action here means both characters that move around a lot and rapid camera effects (e.g. zooming and cutting). The soundtrack was also important in holding a look, with laughter, applause, spirited music, rhyming, alliteration and strange sounds or voices maintaining a look. Children were seen to be more likely to pay attention to segments where characters were women or children. Indeed 'containing children' seems to be a key construct for child viewers (Eke and Croll 1992) perhaps signalling to young viewers that the programme is intended for their viewing. Anderson and his co-workers also drew attention to the concept of attentional inertia and you will have noted that you have been invited to critique this idea above. Subsequent studies of the features of television that elicit orienting responses have been used to suggest that they engage young children in the exploration of novel stimuli presented through the screen. This could be important if the orientating response to some televisual features disrupts the play activities that have been found to be so significant in young children's intellectual development. Schmidt et al. (2008) have explored the impact of background television on young children's play behaviour and they suggest that the impact on young children's play in the home is small, although the impact on their linguistic and cognitive development may be amplified by the amount of background television present in some homes.

Nearly all of the research described above does not look at what children do in their usual everyday settings. Computer screens, like television are most likely to be accessed in the home, Facer et al. (2001) report that very nearly 70 per cent of their respondents had a computer in the home. A survey by Ipsos Mori reported in the Observer (27 July 2008) now suggests that this figure is nearer 90 per cent. We can note that there is some evidence suggesting that on-line and processing capacities are socially distributed (BT 2004) so that the more affluent families have better access to the net and computing technologies. For young children (perhaps 2–7) these are technologies they are keen to use, with video games reported as a common usage with positive and negative consequences (Goswami 2008). As readers we have often found ourselves reading between all the material discussing effects to come to grips with children's capacity to control the technologies of which they are apparently victims. Children's ability to use input devices has been discussed (Revelle et al. 2001) with research contributing to product design and illustrating the social nature of computer-orientated activity. Our own work (Butcher et al. 2002) reported that 4 and 5 year-olds are familiar with a wide range of technological devices and recognize the importance of devices for loading games wear on to various types of hardware. By 7 they are competent users of a wide range of resources, some of which are access controlled by mum and dad and others shared with siblings. Both boys and girls report regular social usage, with girls favouring television and boys games play. The research method asked children to create their own texts using digital cameras and word processing. In the visits to work with the children the construction of the text was a priority for them and suggested that making meaning using contemporary media was a priority for them. The use of YouTube and similar sites by older users suggests the desire to use the media to make and communicate meanings remains a priority.

Reflection

The Ipsos Mori study reported above asked respondents which of the following devices they would keep if they were only allowed to keep one:

- Computer
- Games consoles
- Internet access
- Laptop
- Mobile phone

⇨

- MP3 player
- Not sure
- Television

What would you keep and what would you most readily part with? Can you explain why? Twice as many UK 11–18 year olds in this study would rather just have a mobile than just have a television. What does this tell about their usage of new technologies?

We are presenting a view of young learners who are prepared to use screens as a source of meaning, both in terms of cultural information and of social positioning for themselves and others (Buckingham 2000). We view children as social learners using technology to share meanings, not victims waiting to be eaten by Pacman (Emes 1997). We, like every other writer in the area, can confidently declare that more research is needed.

What ways of being for young children do adults create in contemporary media?

Constructing the child audience

Children's television began when the television service resumed in 1946 at the end of World War II. *Watch with Mother* was introduced in 1950, which included a series of programmes featuring puppets. Oswell (1995) suggested that the adults involved in producing these early programmes were responsible for constructing the child audience:

> Both *Listen with Mother* and *Watch with Mother* did not merely address an audience that already existed. The emergence of these programmes signifies the *invention* of this small audience . . . the distinctiveness and separateness of this audience for broadcasters was a historical invention. (Oswell 1995, p. 37)

So what do these programmes tell us about the way this new audience was constructed?

The very title *Watch with Mother* tells us that children were expected to be supervised by their mother. This concern with presenting models of 'good' mothering, which in this context involved protecting children from television not intended for a young audience, was also apparent in scheduling considerations. There was a period of non-transmission during this period between 6 p.m. and 7 p.m. – the so called 'toddlers' truce' – which was intended as a clear indication that programmes after the closedown were not to be watched by children, and also allowed time for young children to be put to bed. (This in turn has some mirror in the *Bedtime Hour* on CBeebies today, followed by closedown on that channel, which is scheduled between 6 p.m. and 7 p.m., at which point well-parented young children should presumably be tucked up in bed!)

Whose voice?

Reflection

Find some clips from *Watch with Mother* online – try the British Film Institute web site at http://www.screenonline.org.uk/tv/id/445994/index.html

- Who can you see?
- Listen to the way the adults talk. How important is the voice of the narrator?
- Who are the children invited to identify with?
- What actual voice do 'children' have?

The narrators for these early children's television programmes often spoke *for* the child-like puppets as well as *to* them.

> Unlike contemporary makers of pre-school children's television, who recognize the importance of giving children a voice, the BBC in the early 1950s considered it important to set up clear lines of authority between mother and child and to establish childhood as a space spoken and . . . supervised by the mother. (Oswell 1995, p. 41).

The spaces the puppets inhabited were also strictly confined to children's spaces in the home and garden – the outside world did not intrude. The childhood represented by early children's television in the United Kingdom took place in a separate, protected space. This image of a protected, separate audience of young children was part of the public service remit of the BBC; the service felt duty bound to go beyond entertainment and consider what children 'needed'.

These images of childhood now look rather dated to many (although undoubtedly still appealing to some) and certainly to some degree unrepresentative of the lives of the audience even then. So does the design of young children's screen experiences today suggest a shift in the conception of childhood? How are young children represented now?

Reflection

Watch a selection of programmes aimed at young children on weekday early morning television (from 6 a.m.–9 a.m.). Listen to the way the adults talk.

- How important is the voice of the narrator?
- Who are the children invited to identify with?
- What actual voice do they have?

Conceptions of childhood

The way that children are represented on screen gives us some indication of the current conceptions of childhood. At the end of the 1990s, Buckingham and his colleagues (1999, p. 149) interviewed a number of people involved in producing, directing, scripting and researching children's television. They categorized the different ways in which their interviewees discussed their child audience:

- The 'vulnerable' child in need of protection from inappropriate television
- The 'child-centred' discourse which considers what children need and want in terms of stages of development
- The child as a 'social actor' and 'consumer'
- The child as a 'social actor' and as a potential 'citizen'

Buckingham and his colleagues went on to suggest that to some degree these categories can be seen as appearing sequentially, although all of these descriptions still appear in debates around television for young children and there is a great deal of overlap between these categories.

Reflection

Consider the children's programmes you watched in the first two tasks.

- Use Buckingham's categories to help you to identify the way that children are represented in these programmes.
- Do any of the programmes present children at points 3 and 4 on Buckingham's list; as competent, social beings in their own right?

And how do these constructions of childhood fit the 'new' media – what about computers and online activities? For those who primarily view children as vulnerable, the idea of young children using computers is an anathema; it is an activity completely at odds with their vision of what constitutes a 'good' childhood and something that children need protection from. The Alliance for Childhood in the United States is one group which fundamentally disagrees with the use of computers by young children. They argue that the high-tech agenda pushes children to hurry up and become skilled little technicians, experts in 'accessing' other people's answers to narrow, technical questions and manipulating machine-generated images.

> We do not know what the consequences of such a machine-driven education in adulthood will be. But we suspect that they will include a narrower and more shallow range of intellectual insights, a stunting of both social and technical imagination, and a drag on the productivity that stems from imaginative leaps. In short, a high-tech agenda for children seems likely to erode our most precious long – term intellectual reserves — our children's minds. (Cordes and Miller, 1999, pp. 96–97)

This emotive polemic is centred on an essentially romantic view of childhood, and along with that, a view of Information and Communications Technology which suggests that it is too adult, mechanistic and uncreative for children, particularly young children.

However, despite such alarmist predictions, many of the software and online materials provided for young children are very similar to their televisual equivalents. Although the term 'audience' is absent, and there is an expectation of interactivity inherent in the medium, they are often simply multimedia versions of books, television programmes and films already familiar to children. The CBeebies website and the additional stories, colouring sheets to download and songs contained there hardly seem to be the stuff of an infant cultural revolution.

Does children's TV reflect young children's lives?

One television producer interviewed (Buckingham et al. 1999) who commented particularly on the 'child-centred' discourse and how this involved a commitment to protecting children was also keen to emphasize that a concern with children's welfare went beyond this;

> '. . . the duty of care had broader implications, which were not merely protectionist: children were entitled to "a television service of their own" which "reflected" their lives; programme-makers committed to children's broader welfare had a duty to provide such a service – and in this sense caring for children involved a recognition of their autonomy as well as their vulnerability.' (Buckingham et al. 1999, p. 159)

So does children's television 'reflect' their lives? Adults might reasonably expect to turn on the television and see many aspects of their lives represented, whether in the form of drama, documentary or 'reality' television. There is an expectation that all facets of life will be there as a choice for viewers. Older children and teenagers too may expect a degree of this type of representation, although this has not been without controversy. But what about young children's television . . . are their lives really 'reflected'? Or do notions of children as 'vulnerable' and in need of protection preclude this?

Cultural and ethnic diversity

It has become much more common to see cultural and ethnic diversity represented in the characters in television programmes for young children. Programmes in which young children appear, for example, *Teletubbies* and *Nina and the Neurons* routinely include children from a range of ethnic groups. *Sesame Street* was an early pioneer of using both real children from different ethnic backgrounds and multi-coloured puppets in a conscious aim to promote cross-cultural acceptance. Early research on the impact of *Sesame Street* suggested that this was proving successful; white children who watched regularly for two years showed improved positive attitudes towards black and Hispanic people (Bogatz and Ball 1971).

However family films are still prone to portraying stereotyped non-white characters. On the rare occasion where a non-white character is one of the main positive characters, their physical characteristics which mark their ethnic origin (skin tone, eye shape, accent) are presented in a very muted way; they often look and sound almost white (Giroux 1997).

Gender

Cartoons have frequently been criticized for reinforcing gender stereotypes. Thompson and Zerbinos (1997, p. 428), in comparing gender bias in cartoons against similar research from the 1970s found only a slight improvement in terms of representations of work, with only 13 per cent of the female characters having jobs and none of the male characters in a caregiving role. However they also noted positive changes; the female characters were now more independent, assertive, helpful and generally competent (Thompson and Zerbinos 1995).

In an analysis of video games Dietz (1998) found that these contained a similar gender bias:

> Among the entire sample, more than half ignored female representations altogether. Furthermore, if one combines this lack of representation together with examples such as depictions of "Princess What's Her Name", these games demonstrate the value, or lack of, given to women in this society. In most other cases, women were portrayed as victims or as sex objects, but rarely as a positive role model for young girls and boys.

In other types of children's programmes, male characters dominate and although key female characters appear frequently, where there is a lead character it is almost always a male role, for example: *Noddy, Fireman Sam, Postman Pat, Bob the Builder, Rupert Bear*. There are exceptions to this, for example, *Fifi and the Flowertots, Franny's Feet* and *The Little Princess* (interestingly all of which appear on channel 5's *Milkshake*, a commercial station rather than the publicly funded BBC). The claim has often been made that the predominance of male leads is a commercial decision based on the idea that girls will watch 'boys' programmes but that boys will not watch 'girls' programmes (Kline 1995).

Although there have been improvements, family films also frequently demonstrate strong gender stereotyping. *Shrek* is an interesting example; the princess is uncharacteristically feisty and the hero is an ogre but the princess has still been waiting around in a tower to be rescued and willingly consents to being delivered to the prince to be married. Even when a seemingly more traditional ending is diverted to involve the princess marrying the ogre, the theme of the single female only being complete on marrying her 'one true love' continues (Takolander and McCooey 2005). Zipes (1995) notes this persistent theme in Disney productions: '. . . .the disenfranchised or oppressed heroine *must* be rescued by a daring prince. Heterosexual happiness and marriage are always the ultimate goals of the story' (Zipes 1995, p. 111).

Behaviour

However sometimes it is not only the way that programme-makers think about childhood which prevents them from making programmes which reflect children's lives; sometimes there are also problems relating to what young children are able to understand. For example, it would seem reasonable to expect that sometimes the fictional child or child-like characters on screen would behave very badly – it would after all be a rare young viewer who had never at least seen a child hit (or bitten!) by another at a pre-school setting. A constructive response promoting pro-social aims could then follow. It is hard to imagine this type of 'reality' forming part of the vision for children's television but more recently research has suggested that this type of scene is also confusing for pre-school children. Young children often do not understand the link between the antisocial act and the consequences and so take away a strong impression of the antisocial act in isolation rather than taking on board the prosocial message which followed (Mares and Woodward 2001).

Bucking the trend?

But there are other ways of representing the complexity and diversity of children's lives. In the early days of children's television the BBC showed a predominantly middle class, and with it, sanitized version of childhood. In 1978 Grange Hill, aimed at older children, provoked considerable controversy in its portrayal of working class children facing genuinely difficult issues. For many young people this looked a lot more like real life than anything seen previously. Nothing so bold has been attempted for young children although, interestingly, another programme which caused a considerable stir at the time was *Teletubbies*. The main criticism related to the language used – the programme makers aimed to mimic the emergent language their target audience of toddlers would be using rather than use more advanced language to try to help children improve their speech. The character of Dipsy is also particularly important as he mimics children's spatial representations. This business of reflecting aspects of children's lives rather than only trying to educate (although there are elements of that too) certainly courted a great deal of criticism. The breakout films of real children appearing on the *Teletubbies* also feature groups of children from a variety of socio-economic groups as well as different ethnic groups.

Single parent families who, according to a recent report by the Office of National Statistics (ONS 2007) make up nearly one in four families are also beginning to appear on screen, although in a rather understated way. Franny in *Franny's Feet* seems to live with her grandfather and the adult character

Bobby in CBeebies' *Me Too* appears to be a single parent as her child stays at the childminder's house whilst Bobby works cleaning the buses at night. *Me Too* presents an interesting mix in terms of representing children's lives; parents with a range of different jobs and socio-economic groups are represented and the children stay with Granny Murray the childminder whilst their carer is at work. This shows important features of many children's lives but it nonetheless also shows a relentlessly cheerful image of those lives; no child is ever distressed when their carer leaves them at the childminder's, Granny Murray (who is probably in her late 30s, despite being known as 'granny') is extraordinarily and permanently cheerful and all the parents also love their work and never appear hurried or under pressure! How risky would it be to show young children a positive and interesting programme but one which also shows more varied and challenging scenarios and behaviours which will be very familiar to them?

Tackling difficult issues

Sesame Street has occasionally shown itself to be bolder in showing difficulties in children's lives – in some instances *much* bolder. For example, Sesame Workshop produced a pack, including a DVD, for parents and children featuring the Sesame Street muppets, *Talk, Listen, Connect: Helping Families During Military Deployment*, aimed at helping children who had a parent deployed in the Iraq war. This was distributed to military families rather than as a common broadcast, but the aim of using a popular children's television programme to help children with trumatic life events is an interesting one. Since 2002 the South African version of Sesame Street, *Takalani Sesame*, has featured Kami, a muppet who is HIV positive. She is 5 years old and can do all the things a normal 5 year-old can do.

Reflection

Again, consider the early morning programmes aimed at young children that you watched before.

- How much do the child/child-like characters reflect *your* experiences as a child?
- Think about children whose experiences may be very different from your own. Do you think that some of these experiences are reflected in the programmes you watched?
- What sort of childhoods do you think are most successfully represented?

What are the consequences for the young child viewer and the adults around them?

In this third section you will learn about young children's talk about media and *their* constructions of *themselves* as viewers and computer users. They will be seen to be users of a more diverse range of texts than the producers intended and we will consider the consequences of this. Alongside this discussion we will also look at what we can learn from media productions that children have produced. In so doing we will share our interest in children's talk about media and the meanings they share.

What children watch

The ongoing debate about the quality and nature of programming for children often sidesteps the key issue of how much children watch programmes aimed at their age group. Even alarmist reporting about children watching adult programmes and films often assumes that at least the youngest viewers are confined to the programmes aimed at their age group. However Van Noort (1992) in her research with 4 year-olds in two nursery classes found that all the children watched a significant amount of television aimed at older children or adults. When asked about their favourite programmes, the only pre-school programmes mentioned were *Rainbow* and *Spot*; the most popular programmes at both schools were *Neighbours* and *Home and Away*, with a number of children able to discuss the *Nightmare on Elm Street* series of horror films. Most children were able to describe videos that they did not like.

Teacher	What about at home, do you ever watch anything at home that frightens you?
Child	Yeah – you know that film I watched with me dad, we stayed up right late while half past two, right, well you know that man, right, that was in bed wi' that lady and he were trying to kiss her, right, and he were trying to shoot her head off.
T	Oh, and did that frighten you?
C	It frightened me dad.

> *T*   Did it frighten you?
> *C*   Yeah, it did. (Van Noort 1992, p. 279)

A number of authors have suggested that the extent of parents' concern over violent programmes relates strongly to social class. Buckingham (2000) suggests that middle class families are more likely to censor programmes for being too violent. The children studied by Van Noort were largely from working class backgrounds.

The issue of how much choice the children in Van Noort's study were exercising here is a difficult one. The videos that the children were frightened by were often films that their fathers were watching so the children may not have chosen to watch them, although they did report making an active choice *not* to watch by hiding their faces from the screen or by turning the television off or going to bed.

> *T*   Why did you watch it if it was so horrible? Did it frighten you?
> *C*   Yeah, and I scared of it and I went to bed. (Van Noort 1992, p. 280)

However, although the daytime soap operas may also have been on because an older member of the household was watching them, the children did make the active choice to continue to watch them and in school discussed them enthusiastically as favourite programmes. It is difficult to determine whether children described the soap operas as favourite programmes because they are simply often on when children are in the room and children learn to like them or whether it is because the programmes made specifically for their age group are lacking in some way. Perhaps some aspects of the lives presented in these soaps seemed more representative of the lives of their young viewers? Marsh and Millard (2000) suggest that the appeal of soap operas for young children is indeed due to the family-life context which they can relate to and also to some similarities with fairy tales, including the simplistic nature of the characterizations. Soaps also tend to be programmes that the whole family watch and so the social aspect of viewing may be an important part of the children's enjoyment of them.

Children also make active choices to watch programmes aimed at older children and adults in order to gain cultural capital (e.g. Buckingham 1993). So with many children watching programmes aimed at an older demographic, it is clear that the careful efforts of the producers of programmes for young children to present a sanitized, safe, broadly educational and above all *contained* setting for their viewing seem largely obsolete.

Consequences for children

So what are the consequences for children of this use of a much more diverse range of texts? One issue is whether children find programmes aimed at older viewers too frightening. One important determinant of how frightening a programme might be is whether the children think that what they see is real or pretend. If children watch programmes which are intended to frighten adults who understand that they are not real, how much more frightening will they be for young children who think that they *are* real? In Van Noort's study (1992) the children all thought that the daytime soaps, the horror films and the news were real.

> T   Did the man shoot the lady's head off?
> C   Yeah
> T   What did it look like?
> C   All blood everywhere.
> T   How horrible! Was it real? Did it really happen?
> C   Yeah.
> T   Or was it pretend?
> C   No, it really happened. (Van Noort 1992, pp. 279–280)

However the issue of what constitutes 'real' is a difficult one. Is the child's understanding of 'real' the same as the adult's? Or does it relate more to whether it is 'realistic', and/or enacted by people rather than cartoons or puppets? One of the challenges for children is developing and refining their ability to make modality judgements – to be able to watch Holby City and understand that it is not a medical documentary.

Like adults, children will vary in their responses. In Van Noort's study, although most children were scared by violent films, one child reported watching films like this with his father and, 'When asked if watching these films frightened him he said no, and he did not seem frightened'. (Van Noort 1992, p. 281)

Reflection

If you live or work with young children then you may have the opportunity to talk to them about their viewing.

- What television programmes do they describe as favourite programmes?
- How many of these are programmes aimed at their age group?
- Ask them about what is 'real' or 'pretend' but be careful to listen carefully to their reasoning.

Wider implications

A great deal of the discussion in the press over children watc
has centred around whether this has an impact on how v
and become in their own behaviour. Research in this area has
atic due to the difficulty of researching in a real life situation and the challeng-
of trying to establish whether any impacts of viewing are temporary or more
permanent. Huesmann et al. (2003), in their 15-year longitudinal study found
that children who watched violence on television between the ages of 6 and 9
were more likely to be aggressive as adults. However Charlton et al. (2000)
researched the playground behaviours of children living on the Atlantic
island of St. Helenas both before and five years after the introduction of TV
on the island and found little difference. Other studies (e.g. Anderson et al.
2001) have found a slightly higher level of aggression apparent in children who
watched more violent programmes as children but *only* for particular groups
of vulnerable children.

Beyond the research, the debate over the possible impacts of children viewing adult material has also included an active and often passionate media
debate about the wider implications. This is often as much about the consequences for adults as for children; what happens when children step outside
the carefully constructed boundaries that adults have set for them? How
'childlike' can children remain whilst watching adult programming? If we open
the floodgates of adult behaviours to child viewers, will we simultaneously
bring to a premature close the experience of being a child? '... television erodes
the dividing line between childhood and adulthood ... electric media find it
impossible to withhold any secrets. Without secrets, of course, there can be no
such thing as childhood' (Postman 1994, p. 80).

Children's access to computers provokes similar concerns to children's
access to a diverse range of televisual texts. Selwyn's (2003) account of the 'vic-
timized' child computer user – the innocent child just a few clicks away from
online sexually explicit material is very similar to Buckingham's 'vulnerable'
child in need of protection from inappropriate television. Both these representations construct children as passive, weak and in need of protection. Other
accounts of child computer users see them as more active and competent
participants which, although often positive, can also be seen as part of the
slippery slope towards the 'dangerous' child computer user (Selwyn 2003).
In this representation, children are seen as potential deviants who actively seek
out adult games and online materials of a violent and/or sexual nature.

Of course where you find yourself in this debate depends on your conception of childhood; how *do* we expect children to think and behave and does this relate to the real experiences of children or to a need by adults for a place in which to situate the notion of innocence and goodness? And have children's precocious viewing habits really led to a radical change in childhood or are the changes we see just part of the inevitable changes in society? We are reminded of a remark attributed to Caxton (1422–1491) '. . . Sir, all I can say in defence of the printing press is that books are here to stay. We cannot dis-invent them, so we must adapt'.

Each new technological development, whether it be the printing press or the internet, is described as provoking a wave of moral panic relating to the scope children will now have for straying from the cultural spaces currently provided for them. Many of the concerns center around the freedoms inherent in the media – the increased freedom to move easily and intentionally or unintentionally beyond the materials provided for young children, and also the freedom for children to use the media to create materials of their own. If we are asking 'whose childhood is it?', perhaps what we learn from each furore surrounding the most recent technological advances is that each new development provides opportunities to debate the boundaries that adults attempt to set for children. And of course...'The ultimate problem with children it would seem, is their unwillingness to *be* children – at least as defined by adults' (Buckingham et al. 1999, p. 119)

Constructing alternatives – imaginary play and children as producers of media

Children's unwillingness to confine themselves to a passive 'audience' role as defined by adults manifests itself in watching programmes aimed at an older demographic but also in engaging in decidedly *active* representations of all types of viewing in the form of imaginary play and also in becoming media-makers themselves using cameras, camcorders and computers.

Imaginary play

Those who are concerned by young children watching television often cite children's passivity in front of the television as a sign of a generally passive state of mind. The title of Marie Winn's book, *The Plug-in Drug* (2002), headlines this concern, whilst in the text she refers to children as 'television zombies' who watch with a trance-like, 'glazed, vacuous look' (Winn 2002, p. 17).

However others contest this account of children's viewing, asserting that the process is a much more active one. Browne (1999) comments on:

> . . . the *active* way in which these very young children watched television and videos: they danced, sang, asked questions, kissed the screen, attempted to mirror what was happening on the screen, and made effective use of the remote control to ensure that they watched what *they* wanted to watch. The children did not necessarily respond to explicit invitations to 'sing along' or 'join in and clap hands' made by adult presenters on shows such as Playdays or Sesame Street, instead the children made their own decisions about when they wanted to participate and when they wanted to adopt the role of an onlooker. (Browne 1999, p. 1)

Smidt (2001) describes her granddaughter's interaction with television and video:

> She will watch the same video over and over again until she can almost recite the dialogue by heart and has made it her own . . . This is not a passive process but a rapt and highly interactive one. What she is doing is interacting, in her head, with the characters and events depicted.

Evidence for this often lies in the imaginative play which results from this viewing. Children frequently use television characters as part of their play, whether it's the Teenage Mutant Ninja Turtles or the Disney princesses. Smidt (2001) describes her granddaughter's re-enacting the story of *The Secret Garden* with the plastic dinosaurs that she had at hand. And Adams and Moyles (2005) describe how nursery children used building blocks and pretend play to help them to come to terms with the attack on the twin towers on 11 September. These activities do not constitute an exact replication of the original; instead, the children use the televisual stimuli as a starting point. Indeed we are arguing here that children make choices from the media available to them and use these choices to inspire imaginative play. For boys this is often rough and tumble play, and such play is often positioned as unwelcome in nursery / school settings. Bromley (1996) describes how a group of Reception children were allowed to continue to develop a play based on Aladdin, which they had started in the playground. The children took bits of the film that they liked, discarded parts they did not like and added to the plot themselves to develop a vibrant and original production of their own.

Children as producers of media

This image of children actively transforming media for their own purposes has more in common with the third and fourth of Buckingham et al.'s categorizations which show children in a more independent, participatory light as 'social actors' in the form of consumers and potential citizens. It also has similarities with Selwyn's 'natural' child computer user and the 'successful' child computer user. These see children as innately competent at all aspects of ICT, as ICT 'natives' from a very young age.

Marsh (2004) describes how three nursery-aged children worked with webcams to create simple animations. The children were shown how to use the equipment and asked to plan a story then they were left to work independently. The resulting animations were short but complete and followed the plans they had made. Marsh comments:

> The production of such multimodal texts is an important step in understanding the nature and potential of moving image media and is as important to contemporary communicative practices as the print-based activities that are a regular feature of the early years curriculum. (Marsh 2004, p. 41)

Children's media rights

There has been an increasing momentum to recognize children's engagement with contemporary media. The overriding official response to this (DfEE 1997; Byron 2008) has been a concern to 'innoculate' children against any harmful effects of this through legislation aimed at protecting children and through helping to educate children to become skilled consumers both of media products and associated cultural production. The recent Byron Review (2008) makes a number of recommendations, including a voluntary code of practice to restrict availability and access to the internet, better information and education about e-safety and support to enable parents to achieve basic media literacy. The report also recommended that OfSTED should report on e-safety and media literacy in schools. The remit of the review and the emphasis of the report is on how to protect children. This may have influenced the fact that the call for evidence from children was clearly aimed at older children, and in fact of the 346 responses to the children's consultation document, only two were from children aged from 0–7.

One of the key means presented by the Byron Review for achieving e-safety is promoting 'media literacy'. 'Media literacy' is seen as a tool '. . . to empower people with the skills, knowledge and confidence they need to embrace new technology to make the decisions that will protect themselves and their family' (Byron 2008, p. 109). Mercer (1992) takes a wider view than protection and suggests that, 'The emergence of the concept of "media literacy" reflects a growing awareness that children need to be helped to interpret, as well as to appreciate, the products of the mass communications industries.' Certainly, if we think we need to scaffold children's understanding of print literacy it must be similarly important to scaffold their understanding of media literacy.

As Postman pointed out, screen media does not discriminate by age. 'The six-year old and the sixty-year old are equally qualified to experience what television has to offer.' (Postman 1994, p. 84) So if we are to support media literacy, it must surely include the very youngest children and include addressing difficult concepts such as genre, modality (what is 'real'), audience and the intent of advertising. Mercer (1992) emphasizes the role of the teacher in scaffolding children's media experiences in order to, 'offer children access to conceptual frameworks which are part of the cultural knowledge of their society, frameworks through which children can make more sense of their world'.

However, as important as this is, we would argue for a wider view of media literacy again; children need to be writers as well as readers of media. Children's enthusiasm for this is evidenced by the 250 media products sent in by children as part of the Children's Call for Evidence for the Byron Review. These submissions were appreciated but this enthusiasm for being purposeful makers of media rather than simply consumers was not reflected in the report as a whole. If children are to really make sense of their world then this must involve the means to create their own images, presentations, adverts, animations and films.

This creative conception of media literacy is very close to earlier definitions of visual literacy that identify the importance of children's agency in making cultural products:

> To move towards visual literacy is to engage in the process of developing an appropriate visual form, such as a photograph, to represent personal idiosyncratic meanings. This process necessitates an engagement which is best understood as a dialogue between artefact and author, in that it involves expression, response, editing and modification. . . . To engage in this dialogue, children must become

familiar with the cultural, social and personal histories involved and relate these to a wide range of visual texts. (Eke and Taylor, 2000, p. 111)

Buckingham argues that children have a *right* to this level of agency, involvement and creativity.

. . . we would place a central emphasis on children's *rights* rather than simply on their *entitlements*. In other words, we would argue that children should be seen as social actors in their own right rather than as passive recipients of a culture generated by adults on their behalf. This means devising mechanisms for access, democratic accountability and control, through which children are enabled to articulate their *own* needs and concerns as an audience, and to create their own media culture. (Buckingham et al. 1999, p. 75)

This suggests not just a re-evaluation of the importance of media for young children and the nature of media education in schools but a shift in the way we conceptualize childhood. It involves addressing the status of children, valuing them *now* rather than simply as future adults – as 'beings' rather than 'becomings' (Lee 2001) – and expecting them to have views on, and be active participants in, their own lives. In terms of their screen experiences, this would involve providing screen experiences that reflect their lives and facilitating and supporting their active engagement in creating media representations of their own.

Summary

- Young children demonstrate developing skills as viewers and demonstrate active viewing choices through selective attention to the screen. Screen experiences are commonly social rather than isolated.
- Young children are familiar and competent with a large range of technologies.
- Programmes and online material created for young children present a limited voice for children and represent a limited view of childhood.
- There have been improvements in the portrayal of cultural and ethnic diversity, gender, different family arrangements and different socio-economic groups in children's programming, but much needs to be done to counteract stereotypes and to ensure that all children are represented.
- Children respond by accessing a more diverse range of screen experiences than those created for them. This has raised concerns that children are moving beyond the boundaries of childhood that adults have set for them.
- Children's engagement with media requires a more respectful and committed response which should include the right to media education and to the means to become producers of their own media creations.

Recommended Reading

Bazalgette, C. and Buckingham, D. (1995) *In Front of the Children*. London: British Film Institute.

Marsh, J. (1999) Teletubby tales: popular culture and media education, in Marsh, J. and Hallet, E. (eds) *Desirable Literacies: Approaches to Language and Literacy in the Early Years*. London: Sage.

Selwyn, N. (2003) 'Doing IT for the kids': re-examining children, computers and the 'information society', in *Media, Culture & Society*, 25, 3, 351–378.

Bibliography

Adams, S. and Moyles, J. (2005) *Images of Violence: Responding to Children's Representations of the Violence They See*. London: Featherstone Education Ltd.

Anderson, D., Huston, A., Schmitt, K., Linebarger, D. and Wright, J. (2001) Early childhood television viewing and adolescent behaviour: the Recontact Study, in *Monographs of the Society for Research in Child Development*, 66, 1.

Anderson, D. R. and Levin, S. (1976) Young children's attention to 'Sesame Street', *Child Development*, 47, 3, 806–811.

Anderson, D. R. and Lorch, E. P. (1983) Looking at television: action or reaction?, in Bryant, J. and Anderson, D. (eds) *Children's Understanding of Television: Research on Attention and Comprehension*. London: Academic Press.

Bogatz, G. A. and Ball, S. (1971) *The Second Year of Sesame Street: A Continuing Evaluation*. Volume 1. New York: Children's Television Workshop.

British Telecom (sponsoring The Future Foundation) (2004) The Digital Divide in 2005, an independent study conducted for British Telecom. London: British Telecom.

Bromley, H. (1996) 'Did you know that there's no such thing as Never Land?': working with video narratives in the early years, in Hilton, M. (ed.) *Potent Fictions. Children's Literacy and the Challenge of Popular Culture*. London: Routledge.

Browne, N. (1999) *Young Children's Literacy Development and the Role of Televisual Texts*. London: Falmer Press.

Buckingham, D. (1993) *Children Talking Television*. London: Falmer Press.

Buckingham, D. (2000) *After the Death of Childhood*. Cambridge: Polity Press.

Buckingham, D., Davies, H., Jones, K. and Kelley, P. (1999) *Children's Television in Britain: History, Discourse, and Policy*. London: British Film Institute.

Butcher, H., Eke, R. and Lee, M. (2002) Young children and their conceptions of interactivity, in *The Redland Papers*, 9, 40–51.

Byron, T. (2008) Safer Children in a Digital World: The Report of the Byron Review. Available online at: www.dcsf.gov.uk/byronreview/ [Accessed April 8 2009].

Charlton, T., Panting, C., Davie, R., Coles., D., Whitmarch, L. (2000) Children's playground behaviour across five years of broadcast television: a naturalistic study in a remote community, in *Emotional and Behavioural Difficulties*, 5,4, Winter 2000.

Collins, W. A. (1983) Interpretation and inference in children's television viewing, in Bryant, J. and Anderson, D. (eds) *Children's Understanding of Television: Research on Attention and Comprehension.* London: Academic Press.

Cordes, C. and Miller, E. (eds) (1999) Fool's Gold: A Critical Look at Computers in Childhood. Available online at: http://drupal6.allianceforchildhood.org/fools_gold [Accessed April 8 2009].

Dietz, T. L. (1998) An examination of violence and gender role portrayals in video games: implications for gender socialization and aggressive behavior, in *Sex Roles*, 38, 5–6, 1 March 1998, 425–442(18).

DfEE (1997) Preparing for the Information Age: Synoptic Report of the Education Departments' Superhighways Initiative.

Eke, R. and Croll, P. (1992) Television formats and children's classification of their viewing, in *Journal of Educational Television*, 18, 2–3, 97–105.

Eke, R. and Taylor, T. (2000) Arts and information and communications media, in Kear, M. and Callaway, G. *Improving Teaching and Learning in the Arts.* London: Falmer Press.

Emes, C. E. (1997) Is Mr Pac Man eating our children? A review of the effects of video games on children, in *Canadian Journal of Psychiatry*, 42, 4, 409–414.

Facer, K., Furlong, J., Furlong, R. and Sutherland, R. (2001) Home is where the hardware is: young people, the domestic environment and 'access to new technologies', in Hutchby, I. and Moran-Ellis J. *Children, Technology and Culture: The Impacts of Technologies in Children's Everyday Lives.* London: Routledge Falmer.

Gibbons, J., Anderson, D., Smith, R., Field, D. and Fischer, C. (1986) Young children's recall and reconstruction of audio and audiovisual narratives, in *Child Development*, 57, 1014–1023.

Giroux, H. A. (1997) Are Disney movies good for your kids?, in S. R. Steinberg and J. L. Kincheloe (eds) *Kinderculture: The Corporate Construction of Childhood* (pp.53–67). Boulder, CO: Westview, cited in Anderson, Kristin J. (2002) Parents or pop culture?: children's heroes and role models, in *Childhood Education*, Spring 2002.

Goswami, U. (2008) *Byron Review on the Impact of New Technologies on Children: A Research Literature Review: Child Development*, Annex H Safer Children in a Digital World, The report of The Byron Review. Annersley: Department for Children Schools and Families.

Heuyer, G. (1956) Cinema et affectivite, in *L'ecole des parents*, Janvier, 3, 15–27.

Huesamann, L., Moise-Titis, J., Podolski, C., and Eron, L. (2003) Longitudinal relations between children's exposure to TV violence and their aggressive and violent behaviour in young adulthood, in *Developmental Psychology 2003*, 39, 2, 201–221.

Jaglom, L. and Gardner, H. (1981) The pre-school television viewer as anthropologist, in Gardener, H. and Kelly, H. (eds) *New Directions in Child Development: Viewing Children through Television.* San Fransico: Jossey Bass.

Kline, S. (1995) The empire of play: emergent genres of product-based animations, in Bazalgette, C. and Buckingham, D. (1995) *In Front of the Children.* London: British Film Institute.

Lee, N. (2001) *Childhood and Society: Growing up in an Age of Uncertainty*. Buckingham: Open University Press.

Liebert, R. and Sprafkin, J. (1988) *The Early Window: Effects of Television on Children and Youth* (3rd Edition). Oxford: Pergamom Press.

Mares, M. L and Woodard, E. H. (2001) Positive effects of television on children's social interaction: a meta-analysis, in *Entertainment-Education Research Agenda*, February, 12, 19.

Marsh, J. (2004) Moving stories: digital editing in the nursery, in Evans, J. (ed.) *Literacy Moves On: Popular Culture, New Technologies, and Critical Literacy in the Primary Classroom*. London: David Fulton.

Marsh, J. and Millard, E. (2000) *Literacy and Popular Culture: Using Children's Culture in the Classroom*. London: Sage.

Mercer, N. (1992) Teaching, talk, and learning about the media, in Alvarado, M. and Boyd-Barrett, O. (eds) *Media Education, An Introduction*. London: BFI.

ONS (2007) Social Trends 2006. Available online at: www.statistics.gov.uk/socialtrends37/default.asp [Accessed April 8 2009].

Oswell, D. (1995) Watching with mother in the early 1950's, in Bazalgette, C. and Buckingham, D. *In Front of the Children*. London: British Film Institute.

Palmer, P. (1986) *The Lively Audience: A Study of Children around the TV Set*. London: Allen & Unwin.

Postman, N. (1994) *The Disappearance of Childhood*. New York: Vintage Books.

Prout, A. (ed.) (2000) *The Body, Childhood and Society*. Basingstoke: Palgrave Macmillan.

Revelle, G. L., Medoff, L. and Stromenn, E. F. (2001) Interactive technologies research at children's television workshop, in Fisch, S. F. and Truglio, R. T. *G is for Growing*. Mahwah, NJ: Lawrence Erlbaum Associates.

Schmidt, M. E., Pempek, T. A., Kirkovian, H. L., Lund, A. and Anderson D. R. (2008) The effects of background television on the toy play behavior of very young children, in *Child Development*, 79, 1137–1151.

Selwyn, N. (2003) 'Doing IT for the kids': re-examining children, computers and the 'information society', in *Media, Culture & Society*, 25, 3, 351–378.

Smidt, S. (2001) 'All stories that have happy endings have a bad character': A young child responds to televisual texts, in *English in Education*, 35, 2, 25–33 (Summer 2001).

Stein, N. and Glenn, C. (1979) An analysis of story comprehension in elementary school children, in Freedle, R. (ed.) *Advances in Discourse Processes*, Vol. 2. Hillsdale, NJ: Erlbaum.

Takolander, M. and McCooey, D. (2005) 'You can't say no to the Beauty and the Beast': *Shrek and Ideology*, Source: Papers: Explorations into Children's Literature.

Thompson, T. L. and Zerbinos, E. (1995) Gender roles in animated cartoons: Has the picture changed in 20 years?, in *Sex Roles*, 32, 651–673.

Thompson, T. L. and Zerbinos, E. (1997) Television cartoons: do children notice it's a boy's world?, in *Sex Roles*, 37, 415–432.

Van Noort, S. (1992) Nursery school children talking about television, in Alvarado M. and Boyd-Barrett O. (eds) *Media Education: An Introduction* (pp. 274–291). London: BFI.

Walkerdine, V. (1986) Video replay: families, films, and fantasy, in Burgin, V., Donald, J. and Kaplan, C. *Formations of Fantasy*. London: Methuen.

Winn, M. (2002) *The Plug-in Drug*. London: Penguin.

Zipes, J. (1995) Once upon a time beyond Disney: contemporary fairy-tale films for children, in Bazalgette, C. and Buckingham, D. *In Front of the Children*. London: British Film Institute.

Learning Who Can Talk About What in Early Years Settings

John Lee and Richard Eke

Chapter Outline

Key Questions

1. Are all learners equally well equipped to cope with school/setting talk?
2. How can schools/settings assist children in talking to learn?

Beginning to talk, learning to speak

Language acquisition

There is a remarkable agreement amongst linguists, psychologists and those concerned with child development about the rapidity with which children become users of language. There is a keen debate between those who argue a nativist theory of language learning, who argue that children acquire language because they have a biological programme to do so, and those who stress learning and/or interaction, however we will not focus on those debates here. It would be helpful if you checked on the differences between different theories and the consequences of holding them in the way we might plan and implement provision in the early years.

Reflection

- Look up what Chomsky has to say about language acquisition
- Compare this to a behaviourist position and an interaction position

It might be useful to try a basic up-to-date psychology text book for these investigations.

Regardless of the major differences between theorists and researchers, what they all point to is that by about 3 years old the vast majority of children are able to use language in a wide variety of ways and in a wide variety of circumstances. Let us have a brief look at what most children can actually do. Look in the box below for the most common first words that children know and use (Peccie 2005).

Activity

ball	allgone	no
dog	juice	Daddy
give	Mummy	milk
bye-bye	hi	car
dirty	nice	more
cat	yes	this
sit	up	down
baby	stop	put
go	shoe	biscuit

- Now classify these words first by using these categories and then try to create a category system of your own

    1. Naming (Nouns)
    2. Actions/events (Verbs)
    3. Describing/modifying (Modifiers)

Activity—cont'd

- Now decide what you think the meanings of the words are and how they relate to particular contexts? How many different sorts of meanings do you think 3 and under 3-year-olds can make and use with these 'simple' words?

Even these very young children who use single word utterances are creating meanings by using them in grammatically different ways. Did you note that? Depending on how the child says the word 'juice' and in what context, they know whether they are, for example, labelling, making a request or asking a question. See if you can find a recording of children as young as these speaking; if you are fortunate you may know some one this young.

We noted above the rapidity of linguistic development. Almost from birth babies make serious attempts to communicate, the most obvious being the loud cry of discomfort or distress. Very quickly babies learn how to get the attention of their significant others, later they will use language to do that. So even before what is normally seen as the onset of language development babies make language-like utterances which are ascribed meanings by those who care for them. What is important here is that the meanings are made in 'the space between' the carer and the child. In other words carers recognize that even young babies are potential meaning makers and thus children come to understand that they can make meanings that others understand. All this before what is accepted as the onset of language development, usually set at 18 to 28 months, but remember there may be large variations, so some children speak at 12 months others do not until they are 2.

Look at this summary of language development. As you can see it takes what is really a functionalist perspective, a view that children learn to use language by using it in the world. Basically they are learning language in use by using language.

Function	Meaning	Structure
Children's purposes with their language (e.g., make requests, ask questions, make statements).	What children talk about (states, events and relationships) *Meaning* here refers to meaning shown in performance.	The way in which the language is put together (its grammar).

Stage 1

Children's first utterances usually serve three purposes:

- □ to get someone's attention
- □ to direct attention to an object or event
- □ to get something they want

Next, they begin to:

- □ make rudimentary statements (*Bird gone*)
- □ make requests

They then relate objects to other things, places and people (*Daddy car; There Mummy*) as well as to events (*Bird gone*). They talk about the present state of things

They control limited language forms and convey information by intonation, by non-verbal means, or by the listener's shared awareness of the situation.

Many of the remarks at this age are single words, either the names of things, or words such as *there, look, want, more, allgone*. They are often referred to as operators.

Other remarks consist of object name and operator in a two-word combination: *Look Mummy, Daddy gone, There dog*.

Stage 2

At this stage children begin to ask questions; usually *where* questions come first.

Children become concerned with naming and classifying things (frequently asking *wassat?*).

They may begin to talk about locations changing (e.g. people *coming* or *going* or getting *down* or *up*).

They talk simply about the attributes of things (e.g. *hot/cold, big/small, nice; naughty doggy; it cold, Mummy*).

Children's questions often begin with interrogative pronouns (*what, where*) followed by a noun. *where ball? where gone?*

Articles appear before nouns. Basic [subject]+[verb] structure emerges: *It gone, Man run*, or [subject]+[verb]+[object]: *Teddy sweeties* (=*Teddy wants some sweets*).

Stage 3

By now children ask lots of different questions, but often signalling that they **are** questions by intonation alone (*Sally play in garden, Mummy?*).

They express more complex wants in grammatically complex sentences: *I want daddy [to] take it [to] work*.

Children now begin to talk about actions which change the object acted upon (*You dry hands*).

Verbs like *listen* and *know* appear.

Children refer to events in the past and in the future.

Children talk about continuing actions (*He doing it; She still in bed*) and enquire about the state of actions.

The basic sentence structure has expanded: [subject]+[verb]+[object] +[adverb or other element] appears: *You dry hands; A man dig down there.*

Children begin to use auxiliary verbs (*I am going*) and phrases like *in the basket* [preposition]+[article]+[noun].

Stage 4

As children begin to use increasingly complex sentence structures, they also begin to:

- ☐ make a wide range of requests (e.g. *Shall I cut it? Can I do it?*)
- ☐ explain
- ☐ ask for explanations (*Why* questions appear)

Because children are now able to use complex sentence structures, they have flexible language tools for conveying a wide range of meanings.

Perhaps the most striking development is their grasp (language competence) and use (language perform-ance) of abstract verbs like *know* to express mental operations.

Children in this stage begin to express meaning indirectly, replacing imperatives with questions when these suit their purposes better.

As well as saying what they mean, they now have prag-matic understanding, and suit their utterances to the context or situation.

Children by this stage use question forms (*Can I have one?*) and negation (*He doesn't want one*) easily, no longer relying on intonation to signal their intent. They are now able to use auxiliary verbs Children may duplicate modal verbs (*Please* may can).

Children use one part of a sentence to refer to another part – they use (often implied) relative clauses Now they can do this, language is a very flexible means of communica-tion for them.

Stage 5

By now children frequently use language to do all the things they need it for:

- ☐ giving information
- ☐ asking and answering questions of various kinds
- ☐ requesting (directly and indirectly)
- ☐ suggesting
- ☐ offering
- ☐ stating intentions/ asking about those of others

expressing feelings and attitudes and asking about those of others

Children are now able to talk about things hypothetically or conditionally: *If you do that, it'll. . .*

They are able to explain the conditions required for something to happen.: Often they talk about things which are always so – that is, about general states of affairs.

As well as general references to past and future, children now talk about particular times

They are able to estimate the nature of actions or events, e.g., that things are habitual, repetitive or just beginning.

Children are now able to talk about things hypothetically or conditionally: If you do that, it'll...

They are able to explain the conditions required for something to happen: *You've got to switch that on first. . .* Often they talk about things which are always so – that is, about general states of affairs.

They are able to estimate the nature of actions or events, e.g., that things are habitual, repetitive or just beginning.

Source: Adapted from Moore (2002)

This model explains the process of language acquisition. Children will vary individually in when (relative to their peers) they reach each stage, but there is little variation in the *sequence* of language learning. By the end of Stage 5, a child's language is in place and he or she has a basic lexicon (personal vocabulary) of several thousand words. From now on what is learned increasingly depends upon experience and environment – on opportunities to use language and to hear it used, for a wide range of purposes and a wide range of audiences in a wide range of contexts.

Local Pedagogies

Activity

Read these extracts from transcripts of Sophie with her mother. Sophie is 2.4 years old.

Extract 1

> *Sophie*: Me want that
> *Mother*: What is it?
> *Sophie*: *Seen*
> *Mother*: Plasticine?
> *Sophie*: Mmm.

Extract 2

> *Sophie*: Me want to read that
> *Mother*: Okay let's read that
> *Sophie*: Read that. Wrong side
> *Mother*: I think you've got it upside down
> *Sophie*: Look. Look her toe
> *Mother*: I think they're funny shoes actually. Made to look like toes
> *Sophie*: Why?

- How like an everday conversation do you think these extracts are?
- Where is the meaning being made? You will need to think about the child's talk, the adult's talk and the conversation they are having.
- What is the role of the mother here?
- Who is the principal initiator?

Relate these extracts to what you read below about different pedagogies.

Much has been written about the transfer from home to nursery and school but relatively little is made of the new worlds of talk that the children will enter after transfer. Bernstein (Bernstein and Solomon 1999) refers to a rather radical disjuncture between home and school. He argues that when children are at home they are subject to local and tacit pedagogies; a necessarily technical way of identifying sophisticated events. We do not usually use the term pedagogy to describe what is going on in domestic circumstances but here we are thinking about how parents and others are moulding children's minds and perceptions by the way they use language with them. How can talk shape consciousness? Remember talk is one social activity – it is always related to contexts and social relations. When Bernstein talks about local pedagogy he has in mind those many occasions when parents and other adults consciously instruct children so:

> Local pedagogic discourse . . . regulates the process of cultural reproduction at the level of the initial contextualising of culture, essentially in the family and in peer group relations. (Bernstein 1990, p.194)

This pedagogy establishes who we are and what we are, it teaches us our social position and the kind of social relationships we can easily enter into.

For example, instructions such 'Ask before you leave the table,' or, 'Don't talk with your mouthful,' establish for the child social relationships and what is or is not permissible. You will be able to think of many more. This kind of pedagogy is more easily aligned with the official pedagogy that children later encounter outside the home. But this is not always the case; some local pedagogies may not line up so easily and lead to resistance rather than compliance with the official pedagogy of schooling. Some children might get instructions such as – 'Just tell the housekeeper to do it Jemima', or 'No the servants do that' – how do you think these children might respond to a question like 'Would you like to tidy the bookshelf?'

As important is the idea of a tacit pedagogy:

> The tacit is a pedagogic relation where initiation, modification, development or change of knowledge, conduct or practice occurs, where neither of the members may be aware of it. Here the meanings are non-linguistic, condensed and context dependent . . . (Bernstein and Solomon 1999, p. 267)

There are things that adults do with children which they do not consciously select, you might describe it as automatic such as taking the child's hand when leaving the park and entering the road. This is usually accompanied by the utterances, 'give me your hand' or 'hold hands'. The words are more typically used if the child is out of reach, otherwise the pedagogy is an unspoken action.

All children enter educational settings having experienced tacit pedagogy, the very fact that it is tacit implies they not full aware of its nature. While there are in schools some traces of tacit pedagogy, they are almost as diluted as the chemicals put into homeopathic remedies. In addition to this they have plenty of experience of local pedagogies, they have been taught and shaped at home and occasionally in the community. In brief they know what it is like to be instructed and know that adults want them to meet certain targets or goals. If the goals and the way they have been shaped to meet these goals lines up easily with the official pedagogy they have an advantage, what has been called cultural subsidy.

Communicative competence

As children develop they begin to make longer utterances moving from single words to two or more. As they grow they become more and more competent in their use of language. This is not just lexical and grammatical competence, it is about more than this. They develop what Del Hymes (1972) calls communicative competence. This is the capacity to recognize what kinds of language and other things are needed in particular circumstances. Children rapidly develop communicative competence; in nurseries and schools they treat the teacher as trusted manager, and talk to her in an appropriate manner. You have probably noticed that they are still developing and on occasions will call the teacher, mum or mummy or mammy depending on where they come from. This is not simply a misuse of a word but a confusion about the circumstances the child is in, the social relationships of home and school are different but here are aligned. Children will show they recognize this and make a joke about it when they realize what they have done. 'Oh Mr Lee I've just called you mum and you're a man' giggles the child. As we develop our story you will see how important the idea of communicative competence is and how it is related to very important pedagogical concepts. When children enter educational establishments they meet new and different varieties of language, pedagogic language.

Walking wi' scholars – educationists' responses to pre-school talk

Official pedagogy

In previous chapters you have read about how the early years has been officially segmented by age, so we now have children grouped as 0 to 3 years and 3 plus. The age of 3 is now the watershed established by the state, the age at which children encounter a more formal pedagogy, one that becomes even more formalized as they proceed. You have also learnt how, over time a "national" curriculum for early years has been imposed and how it is monitored through the nuclear weapon of OfSTED inspection. You will also have noted how increased resources for early years have been accompanied by increased regulation of workers in the sector. You might want to reflect on how this increased regulation and inspection might impact on the experiences of young children.

We showed you earlier how most 3 year-olds are, in Hymes' (1972) term, 'communicatively competent'. This means they now have firmly established their own language but more importantly know how it functions and thus are able to learn independently, socially and with the guidance of adults. In brief they know that they can learn new things and talk about them and we can say that through that talk even newer concepts are developed. Almost all rising 4-year-olds in England are now in educational establishments, many in schools, although over time it is likely they will be in Children's Centres. The children's growing communicative competence means they can enter an official pedadgogical world which hopes to shape their consciousness and produce an ideal pupil identity; this identity will be the site of struggle throughout their schooling.

In earlier chapters you have read about play. Our focus will be on talk but as you know, play and talk are symbiotic. When the child enters the institution her/his talk competence is defined less by what the child can actually say and do and more by the state's definition of what the child needs or should have. We have moved from the realm of local pedagogy, with all its subtle variations, to the realm of official pedagogy, which over the past has been the subject of severe regulation by the central government. This began with the Literacy and Numeracy strategies in primary schools and then spread across the curriculum with the Primary National Strategy in 2003 and across age groups with publications directed at the curriculum for the Early Years Foundation

Stage in 2007. This has not always been the case; in the past teachers and perhaps particularly nursery teachers were less centrally directed and had the propensity to develop different versions of pedagogy. They were also in a position where they could engage children in the defining of what counted as knowledge; they were in a position to respond confidently to children's agendas. They did not have to worry whether or not the children's concerns fitted the official curriculum.

Activity

- Talk with a worker in an early years setting and ask how they decide what activities the children will engage with next week.
- Discuss what you have found out with others in your group. It would be useful to find out from each other whether official documents were mentioned and whether children's development was mentioned?

Diverse settings

Let us look at some examples of early years work which are not so subject to central regulation or locked into an official curriculum. You will have read about Steiner and it may be that you attended a Steiner school – if the latter, what we now describe will be familiar to you. Three to four-year-olds in Steiner (Waldorf) Schools are given the opportunity to explore and engage with natural things. They play independently with sticks, mud and leaves. Following Steiner's philosophy they come to know these things and their properties through personal experience not through instruction. There is no expectation that they will all have learned the same things in the same way. Instruction by teachers does not happen in Steiner schools until the children are at least 7; they have to have developed some adult teeth. Even then the instruction tries to take account of what the children want to know rather than simply defining it for them.

In Scotland there is less pressure on teachers to deliver an official curriculum in a prescribed manner. This means that early years teachers and workers are less constrained and are able to respond to the interests of the children. Look at this example in which the head of the nursery, Annie, is talking to a pupil about an earthquake in Pakistan. Before she joined the conversation she sought permission to engage.

James (Pupil): Maybe we can help the people in 'Pakistani'

Annie (Head): You would like to help them? How can we do this?

James: I know I have a good idea. Thunderbirds could help.

Annie: That sounds like a good idea. How can we do this?

James: I know. I have Thunderbirds at my house, its 5,4,3,2,1, Thunderbirds are go!

Annie: Good. How can they help us?

James: Well, they're not real, Annie

Annie: Oh! So that won't work then?

James: No, but I have another good idea. I could take some money from my piggy bank and send it to them.

Annie: Well, James, I think that's a very kind thing to do and if you take some money from your piggy bank, I'll give you some money from my purse to send also.

James: Well, not all the money from my new bank, just a little.

Annie: Of course I'm not giving you all the money from my purse, but I will give some of it. I'm wondering how we are going to get this money to people in Pakistan. (Kinney and Wharton 2008, p. 25)

What we can see here is that this is a proper conversation, unlike many of the verbal interactions between teachers and pupils. Notice the absence of any demands by Annie for James to demonstrate that he has acquired some predefined curriculum knowledge. She has earlier asked him how he knew about plate tectonics and he said that he saw it 'on the telly and heard it on the radio in the car'. There is a sense of equality between the two – James' suggestions are treated very seriously. Annie doesn't just dismiss the Thunderbirds suggestion, she waits for James to explain why it won't work; she leaves him the space to come to his own conclusions. In the case of the money she reassures him that he does not have to give everything and uses herself as an example. There is no sense of urgency to meet the demands of a curriculum; no ideas have to be 'parked for later' in order to get through the demands of an official curriculum. What we have here is a real example of what Siraj Blatchford calls sustained shared thinking. This idea has been adopted and adapted by the authors of the Practice Guidance for the Early Years Foundation Stage which we now turn to.

The Early Years Foundation Stage – Practice Guidance

Government has not been shy of enshrining things in law that were previously considered to be matters of educational principles and arguments.

> The EYFS is given legal force through an order made under the act (Child Care Act 2006) . . . and applies to 'maintained schools; non-maintained schools, independent schools and child care registered by OfSTED.' (DfES 2007, 7, p. 8)

Accompanying the Statutory Framework is an extensive guidance document containing 'essential advice and guidance for all practitioners working with children from birth to five' (Preface to the Early Years Foundation Stage package). This guidance then is not just guidance. You may seek guidance on how to get to Cork but decide to reject the straight forward route on the grounds that you want to visit the Puck Fair, but the document makes clear that the guidance applies and should be treated as having the force of law. The guidance document is part of a package which combines the statutory requirements with supplementary advice and guidance. As a result of this, the guidance has a quasi legal status and what is embodied in it becomes the 'official definition' and description of knowledge and skills to be acquired by children. An example of this is the way in which the idea of sustained shared thinking has been embedded in the official curriculum but in doing that the writers have radically changed what it means in both theory and practice.

Siraj-Blatchford and Sylva (2004, p. 720) in talking about sustained and shared thinking say the following with respect to children's cognitive development.

> The cognitive construction in this case would be *mutual* where each party engages with the understanding of the other and learning is achieved through a process of reflexive co-construction. (our emphasis)

The official discourse reads subtly differently.

> Adults are aware of the children's interests and understandings and adults and children work together to develop and idea or skill. (DfES 2007, p. 9)

Seemingly small changes in vocabulary are very important. 'Awareness of' leaves the adult as the arbiter of what is worthy of further development. This is very different from the notion of mutuality and co-construction; in this case the underlying principle is one of equality. Further, what is worthy of grasping on to in the child's interests is defined in the document and ultimately will be formally assessed through the 117 points on the assessment scales. This is the EYFS profile which determines what the child knows on entry to the reception stage. The power of prescribed assessment means that the adults are only likely to engage in sustained dialogue with children when it matches what is required by the official curriculum. In this process the child is wrapped up in the official pedagogy, which we discussed above. The combination of an official curriculum with an official pedagogy produces ways of talking and learning that are most likely to exclude both the way of talking and the existing knowledge of those least well adapted to 'schooling'. In short the official curriculum is the only knowledge worthy of discussion.

Reflection

- What do you think the differences are between a child in Scotland raising an idea and one in England?
- When you think about this read the Practice Guidance and some description of the Reggio Emilia approach. Ask yourself who has to listen? Who controls what is worth talking about?
- Look for other examples to illuminate how things might go.

We have used the terms official pedagogy and official curriculum, both of which come from the work of Basil Bernstein. Bernstein wanted to show how education and schooling sought to shape the consciousness of children through its practices and its definition of what counts as valuable knowledge and skills. If you look back to the short extract from Scotland you will see how the teacher treats the child as a thinking human being. She recognizes the child has a mind. The kind of pedagogy she uses is much closer to what is called local or even tacit than official. In the case of the topic discussed you can see it comes from the mind of the child not some prescribed official document. As Kinney and Wharton (op. cit.) note the conversation is driven by the child's compassion and not the complex idea of plate tectonics. How is this different from the current situation in England?

The documents we have referred to establish an official curriculum for the Early Years. What is to be learnt is expressed not just in description but as assessment outcomes. The knowledge in Bernstein's terms is strongly classified, an important idea in any discussion of education and schooling. What do we mean by classification? We put it a little simplistically here. First, classification means that some one or some institution, in this case the government, has the power to decide what should be covered and has the power to ensure that it happens. Second, knowledge is defined in such a way that it is compartmentalized, separated. For example in the statutory document Communication, Language and Literacy is separated into the compartments, 'Language for communication and thinking', 'Linking sounds and letters', 'Reading' and

'Writing'. Think back to your own schooling; we are sure you will remember how the different curriculum subjects were separated and even when a connection was clear it was not alluded to.

Reflection

- When you saw the title of this section, 'Walking wi' scholars' what did you think it meant? Having read the section do you still think this?

You might have recognized it as a dialect-you would have been right. You also might have thought of it as something young children and their families do. It's actually literal Lancashire dialect and refers to school pupils as scholars and at Whitsuntide the scholars walked in processions of denominational witness. Here it serves to remind us how language, context and meaning are bound up with each other.

Scholars entering school

The big claim of the EYFS is that it will lay a secure foundation for future learning and give parents confidence in the quality of the setting they choose. These kinds of claims for high quality early years provision are not unusual and you will probably have encountered such claims for other types of provision such the American High/Scope model (see Chapter 1). What we have indicated to you is that rather than laying a foundation what we have is an early practice of what is to come. In other words children learn very early what counts as talk, who can talk and what counts as knowledge (what is worth talking about). By the time children in England join a reception class, during the year in which they have their fifth birthday many already know that their ideas are not significant unless they match the teachers' agenda. What this means is those children shortly after their fourth birthday (rising 5s), are moved into formal schooling in contrast with most of the rest of the developed world. Let us now turn to talking and learning in some reception classes.

Teacher language and pupil identity

We asked teachers to video record samples of their lessons over a period of one year. At the conclusion of the research activity we had 19 transcriptions of lessons in reception classes. The teachers were asked to record lessons in which they were working with the whole reception class or a reception group, mostly this occurred in the morning. This process enabled the teachers to choose the episodes they wanted to represent to us; they chose what for them was valid as reception practice particularly in mathematics and literacy. When we examined the transcripts we had to bear in mind in our analysis that the teachers' work was caught up in the national strategies.

Many children in reception classes were familiar with conventions of talk in large or whole groups. Until the advent of the national strategies after 1997, talking in whole groups was rather different. The most common use of whole class talk was social and this covered a variety of uses. For example the distribution of milk and snacks where the children sat together and selected children served their peers. Story time, a daily event in which children were encouraged to enjoy a story read by the teacher – at times they would request one they had previously enjoyed. Activities that could be lined up with curriculum provision such as P. E., dance, educational television and singing together were common practices. What you will see from our selection of transcripts and what you may have seen in schools is that whole class discussion now takes the form of instruction to meet the demands of a prescribed curriculum. The most usual organization for this is that the children sit in a corner of the room on a carpet and the teacher sits on a chair facing them. The teacher invariably introduces the topic and directs the talk. This means that teachers develop a signalling set of utterances which the children recognize as requiring specified responses; these signals also establish that the teacher and the children share a mode of working. Here are some examples from our transcripts; they come from the beginnings of a range of different lessons.

Lesson 1 literacy

Teacher: 'Right. Let me see if you look ready. Well done Lauren. Jasmine your head/ good girl thank you right. We've got another book this week what can you tell me about the book this week?'

Lesson 2 literacy

Teacher: Well done Oscar thumbs up to you. Well done Sharday. Well done George. George put your hands away you don't need to be touching anyone. Helen

Child: Sir

Teacher: That's fine put your hands down thank you're well done Hetty well done.

Barbara: Thumbs up to you Tommy you can see it's circle time you can come and join us now. Today for our literacy activity does anyone know . . .?

Lesson 3 literacy with ICT

The children are singing and get quieter.

Teacher: Looking up when your voices are away and you're ready please look at me now sit by me then good girl well done hands smiling Oscar well done Sharday

> come and I will speak with her Sharday can you just move a little bit just *come in I want her to sit next to me keep going because I want her to be close to me at the moment because she's just come in Sharday keep going that's it brilliant.*

At the beginning of this chapter we drew your attention to the differences between talk at home and school talk, the differences between local and official pedagogy. These extracts are all from the opening of whole class/group lessons – look how strange the language use is. We can identify some typical usages that signal what is going to be required. These signals also establish order and work practices. This kind of teacher language is commonly called contingency management; it's about learning how to be a pupil not learning a subject. What is being established is what Bernstein calls the pupil identity, the more compliant the pupil is to the teacher's direction the more her/his identity lines up with the demands of schooling. Notice how the teacher directs attention to named pupils praising them, 'well done', 'good girl' and 'that's fine'. The teacher is not only praising the individual but drawing the class's attention to the required behaviour. There is also an interesting example of a sort of secret shared signal 'thumbs up' that serves the same purpose. This talk is the talk of the official pedagogy; to be successful pupils have to learn it. Notice how they have no space to respond except in the required manner. We noted above that the EYFS is orientated towards children knowing about this strange usage and accepting it as meaningful before they enter the reception stage. Section 3 of the statutory framework states under the welfare requirements,

> Children's behaviour must be managed effectively and in a manner appropriate for their stage of development and particular individual needs (DfES 2007, p. 19)

The requirement is for an effective behaviour management policy that is future orientated so as well as keeping children safe, what is enjoined is that they learn how to adapt to school as quickly as possible and part of that is understanding the strange signal language above.

What counts as knowledge

After the introductory signals this literacy class proceeds in the following manner.

> *Teacher:* Our spelling and we are particularly going to be looking at the medial vowel sound. Who can tell me which letter is the medial vowel sound, is it the first letter, the initial letter sound, the middle sound, what the medial vowel sound,

Child: The middle

Teacher: The middle that's right, so we are going to be really listening out on this game *today to see if you can tell me what the medial vowel is. . . .*

Here is an example from mathematics.

Teacher: Right OK we're going to do our maths this morning. . . .right I want Joe to tell *me how many children are going to have a hot dinner today.*

Joe: 1,2,3,4

Teacher: Right can you come and write number four for me please Joe and I want Jez to tell me how many people are going to have packed lunch . . . going to count them up for me Jez please.

Jez: 1,2,3,4,5,6,7,8,9,10,11,12,13,14

Teacher: Smashing right give it to Jez and Jez can write 14, was it 14 Jez.

Here we have two examples of official knowledge. In the first extract we can see how the teacher classifies that knowledge making it very different from the commonsense or everyday knowledge the pupils have. She makes use of a highly technical language which has been well assimilated by the pupils. She gives the pupils immediate feedback confirming that they are able to respond correctly, what she is also doing is confirming they understand the way this knowledge is technically described and thus how its strong classification can be made transparent. In the second extract the teacher begins by using common classroom knowledge, the need to count who eats what. He then moves that on into classified mathematical knowledge by getting the pupils not simply to count but to record it in a mathematical manner. Like the first teacher he gives immediate feedback that confirms that proper mathematical ways and notation have been used and both are accurate. The strong classification is made at the beginning; the pupils are told they are 'doing maths' and it's then confirmed they are doing it appropriately. Here you can see two rather different ways in which the idea of classification is made manifest to the pupils.

Closely related to the way knowledge is classified and framed are the codes that teachers and pupils use to transmit knowledge. Following Bernstein's powerful explanatory theory we would expect that in the classroom when the teacher is delivering formal school knowledge she would use language that we can identify as elaborate code. Here the children are discussing the initial consonant 'z' and as part of that are discussing a book they have shared.

Teacher: . . . What's Zippy doing now?

Pupil: He's eating grass.

Teacher: He's eating grass is he? Who do think this person is here? Neil?

Neil: The man

Teacher: Is it the man – He's a zookeeper. He's the person who looks after all the animals who live in the zoo.

Shortly afterwards this interchange occurs.

Teacher: . . . Who can we see in this picture now? John, who is this? July?

July: A snake and a man

Teacher: Yes it's a snake and I think the zookeeper is looking after her.

The teacher is asking assisting questions (questions intended to promote new thinking) which are context bound and she also picks the child she wants to speak (nominates the speaker) but what she wants is the use of elaborate code which is not context dependent. The pupils' use of 'the man' demonstrates how they are using the context, everyone can see and share the text. For them the use of restricted code is logical since there is no possible ambiguity. In contrast the teacher is eager to establish through feedback a meaning that can be abstracted for the context by specifying the role 'the man' has, he is a 'zookeeper' and as such shares universal traits with all other 'zookeepers'.

In this brief extract you can see the teacher trying to get the children to identify objects, to use phonics and to explain what the objects are for. She is attempting to move the children from commonsense knowledge to curriculum knowledge.

Pupil: Jewellery

Teacher: I brought something else in from home. I wear this to school sometimes if it's a little bit chilly. I wonder what this can be. What does it do? Do you know?

Pupil: T shirt

Teacher: Not quite a T shirt a bit like one but it keeps me warmer than a T shirt What do you think JP?

JP: Jacket

Teacher: Might be a jacket some of you have got a jacket on.

Pupil: *Shirt*

Pupil: *Jumper*

Teacher: Jumper and jacket fantastic. Does anyone know what someone who is clever would do with these. (Produces three fabric balls) What might they do with these? Chrissy? What might they do with these? What do they do with these?

Chrissy: *They go like that* (demonstrates juggling)

Teacher: You're quite right you know what they are going to do but not quite the right word. Do you know Brittany

Brittany: To juggle with

Activity

- Read the short transcript and try to identify when the teacher is attempting to move the pupils from commonsense knowledge to curriculum knowledge.
- How does she draw on the pupils' commonsense knowledge?
- What is the curriculum knowledge she is trying to transmit?
- In your experience have you encountered similar sequences of verbal interaction? How closely do they fit the one above?
- Could this ever be a social conversation

In the extract immediately above you can see how the teacher is playing a well known teacher game called, 'Guess what is in my head?' (Young 1992). You will probably remember this happening to you when you were at school and will undoubtedly have encountered it if you have visited a primary school classroom for even a short period of time.

We began with an account of how children learn or acquire language and we showed you how there is no agreement amongst researchers as to how the process operates. You can see that we have taken a functionalist view of development and shown how children learn to make meaning through the interactions they have with others. This is an important stance to take because it enables us to identify how children learn to use the strange language that goes with formal pedagogy. In doing that we introduced you to the important difference between local pedagogy and official pedagogy by using some of the work of Basil Bernstein. Another important distinction we have introduced you to is that between commonsense knowledge and curriculum knowledge, and the way in which teachers working with children move between one and the other as they seek to teach children curriculum knowledge. In our discussion of pre-school work we showed you how children's knowledge and interests could be prioritized but we went on to show how official documents overlay these practices and effectively seek to define and determine what children's interests should be. In effect these documents restrict the space that children and teachers can explore. Once children enter reception classes then what counts as significant knowledge is very much prescribed. In showing this we drew on the work of Basil Bernstein. We have shown you how curriculum knowledge is strongly classified and framed and how his idea of the use of restricted and elaborate code is related to that. One result of this is that children routinely confuse official school language use with ordinary language use as the teachers try to include children's commonsense knowledge in curriculum knowledge. It is as if children's talk is no longer their own; it is subject to their teachers' response to the downward pressure of policy makers. Official documents seek to define and describe what talk should be used and thus both children and teachers are caught in this web. Only children who master the appropriate language form will have easy access to school knowledge and will thus be successful. It is a sad fact of our system and of the systems in all other developed countries that working-class children are the least likely to gain this mastery.

Summary

1. Children learn language by using language
2. Talking with caring adults and each other is the key to children's language acquisition.
3. Children's varied home experiences mean that they engage in distinctive talk that is tacitly educative.
4. Pedagogy in early years settings can empower and sustain children through dialogue.
5. As children get older the pedagogic imposition of 'outcomes to be covered' presses on children's dialogue.

    5.1. Children become members of larger groups where language is used to forge common sense knowledge into school knowledge
    5.2. Working class children are currently least likely to be successful in making the transition to this school language use.

Recommended Reading

Siraj-Blatchford, I. and Sylva, K. (2004) Researching pedagogy in English pre-schools, in *British Educational Research Journal*, 30, 5, 713–730.

Kinney, L. and Wharton, P. (2008) *An Encounter with Reggio Emilia: Children's Early Learning Made Visible*. Abingdon: Routledge.

Peccei, J. S (2006) *Child Language: A Resource Book for Students*. London: Routledge.

Bibliography

Bernstein, B. (1990) *Class, Codes and Control*. Vol. IV. The Structuring of Pedagogic Discourse. London: Routledge.

Bernstein, B. and Solomon, J. (1999) Pedagogy, identity and the construction of a theory of symbolic control: Basil Bernstein questioned by Joseph Solomon, in *British Journal of Sociology of Education*, 20, 2, 265–279.

DfES (2007) Statutory Framework for the Early Years Foundation Stage [online]. Available at: http://www.standards.dfes.gov.uk/primary/publications/foundation_stage/eyfs/ [Accessed 14 August 2008].

Hymes, D. (1972) Toward ethnographies of communication: the analysis of communication events, in Giglioli, P. (ed.), *Language and Social Context*. Harmondsworth: Penguin.

Kinney, L. and Wharton, P. (2008) *An Encounter with Reggio Emilia: Children's Early Learning Made Visible*. Abingdon: Routledge.

Moore, A. (2002), *Stages of early language acquisition*. Available online at http://www.teachit.co.uk/armoore/lang/acquisition.htm#stages [Accessed 8 April 2009].

Peccei, J. S. (2005) *Child Language: A Resource Book for Students*. London: Routledge.

Siraj-Blatchford, I. and Sylva, K. (2004) Researching pedagogy in English pre-Schools, in *British Educational Research Journal*, 30, 5, 713–730.

Young, R. (1992) *Critical Theory and Classroom Talk*. Clevedon: Multilingual Matters.

Children Representing Experience

Richard Eke and John Lee

Key Questions

1. What importance has been attached to young children's representations ?
2. Why is their mark making so important?
3. How is children's mark making being redefined?

Introduction

Before we begin let us remind ourselves that humans seem to have always represented their experiences; representation can be seen as almost as fundamental as speech in defining humanness. You will be well aware of the way in which humans have represented experience long before writing or any other conventional form of representing and recording happened. Think about the cave paintings that have been found in Western Europe and how they seem to show us how people lived so long ago. Perhaps more dramatically we can see in Australia how paintings represent not just physical reality but the spiritual reality of individuals and groups. When you think about how children develop their representational skills and how they use symbols remember they stand in this long line of human development.

Despite a long tradition of institutional provision for early years, children, pedagogy and syllabus content remain subjects of fierce debate. Even so there is a consensus around the importance and value of young children's representations and the necessity for first hand experience. These emphases are almost as old as the idea of early years provision. We will now look at some of the practices recommended by nineteenth century advocates of early years education, what used to be called doctrines of the great educators. Let us look briefly at what some pioneers/seminal thinkers about young children and education have to say. We will not here try to present a definitive account of those we appeal to, not least because often their ideas are confused and contradictory.

Pestalozzi

Pestalozzi (1746–1827) argued for the essential humanity of children. He believed that education demanding submission and rote learning was wrong; rather the child should be encouraged to develop from within. In arguing this he also stated that discipline was essential, that the child should learn by being disciplined. His concern was to get children to represent objects through drawing and he developed a series of lessons to teach drawing such that children would have the tools with which to draw objects. The teacher first teaches the children to draw horizontal and then vertical lines, the teacher demonstrates and the child imitates. Later other lines are taught. What Pestalozzi was doing was not teaching academic drawing as an end in itself but providing a discipline through which the child could successfully represent the world. Pestalozzi stressed that the child develops and thus what is required is spontaneity and not a rigid programme. He opposed the idea that teachers could make the child into an image required by someone else. Unfortunately his drawing lessons and the use of objects have been misunderstood as rigid programmes rather than the tools by which the child could represent its own humanity, its own place in its own world.

Froebel

Froebel (1782–1852) a follower of Pestalozzi had the same concerns about the nature of development. He argued that play was natural and essential to the development of the human spirit. He identified what he called gifts – simple objects that help the child to explore and represent the world. Like Pestalozzi he was concerned to equip the child with the tools to make representation and like Pestalozzi developed a series of suggested activities some of which we can recognize in today's classrooms. For instance he encouraged children to use colours sequentially beginning with the primary colours and he also encouraged them to represent in drawings the gifts he described. In the case of this kind of representation Froebel goes beyond drawing to things such as weaving and making three-dimensional representations. Both of them believed that what was happening was that the child was representing inner experience as well as the self in the world.

Two other nineteenth-century figures are still influential in early childhood education.

Steiner

The first of these two figures, Rudolph Steiner (1861–1925), like Pestalozzi and Froebel, argued that the developing child was a seed that needed nurture not training. His theories are interesting and complex but we are not going to present them in full, here our concern is with representation. Steiner puts the child from 0 to 7 in the way of the natural world – mud, sticks, stones, wool and so on are the kinds of things the child is encouraged to explore and use. The earliest representations can be seen as the sort of patterns a child makes with sticks and stones. A little later the child is encouraged to draw but is not taught drawing in the way Pestalozzi did. Steiner argues that by letting the child represent its own world in its own way the quality of drawing will be more imaginative and will develop to become more detailed and communicative.

Montessori

Finally we come to Madame Montessori (1870–1952). Like those discussed above she was convinced of the developmental potential of all children. She sought to make them independent and self-sufficient. Although like Steiner she firmly believed children should encounter natural materials she created structured materials such wooden blocks to engage the child in play. This kind of play led the child to explore and then represent aspects of the world through a variety of means both two-dimensional and three-dimensional. What is key to this, as it is for Pestalozzi, Froebel and Steiner, is playfulness; the child is enabled to be spontaneous and not captured in some imposed programme.

Montessori's teacher is the silent presence, there to help and guide but not direct; a startling contrast to the way that early years teachers are now directed to behave. For her and the others, what is required is close observation of children and their activities.

Early mark making

You will have seen how once children can manipulate objects they use them to represent things. They create a symbolic order where things stand for other things and they later use those things to represent what has happened; they can use them to tell a sort of story of past actions. Alongside this children begin to explore how to make marks using their hands and/or things that will make marks. Marks made in sand using fingers are ephemeral but nonetheless have meaning for the child. Our problem is that we always want to treat marks as being relatively permanent so these early marks are often not recognized for what they are. If you look carefully at what the child does you will see that the finger or fingers trace deliberate patterns and that the child's concentration, although short, is always intense. We are all more familiar with the marks that children make using crayons or pencils or paints because they are more familiar ways of making meaningful marks to we adults.

Even so we may have tendency to ignore some marks because they don't seem to fit our view of development, either of meaning or of 'art'. For example Eng (cited in Athey 1990), a pioneer of the study of children's drawing 'attributed no importance' to her case study child's production of her first mark – a vertical line – because she was convinced that drawing began with scribble. What you will have seen is that children make sequences and successions of marks and that even if we find them mysterious they have meaning. There is now an established scholarly tradition that traces Western children's mark making from early scribble onwards. This tradition includes writers interested

Table 7.1

Scholar	Focus of interest/research
Goodenough F. 1926	Measurement of intelligence through children's drawing
Eng H. 1931	Charts the pictorial development of one child
Piaget J. & Inhelder B. 1956	Child's conception of space as revealed by drawings
Harris D.B. 1963	Drawings as measuring intellectual maturity
Kellogg R. 1969	Sequence of pictorial development
Arnheim R. 1972	Relationship of thought to art, importance of the tool
Goodnow J. 1977	Development and nature of drawing relationship to thought

in the development of pictorial representation, particularly shown by the increasing use of perspective, and scholars interested in the way that representation is a demonstration of thought and thus can be used to show how thinking develops. The table below shows a few of the more well known scholars in the field and the dates they published their first seminal book.

For some of these writers the drawing and painting by children is in itself an intellectual activity, while for others children's marks mirror their intellectual activity or capacity. For the last 80 years or so those who have studied children's mark making have established clear links between children's minds being at work and their work making marks.

Activity

Find some examples of children's marks and drawings, try to get some from a fridge door and some from a playgroup or a nursery.

- Can you tell how old the children are from the drawings alone?
- What do you think the drawings represent?
- If there is adult writing on them compare what that says with what you think.

What you will have observed is that children make a variety of marks and that they develop some consistency over time. You will have noted how much enjoyment children derive from the process and how eager they are to share their marks with others, particularly significant adults. No fridge in the home of a young child should be considered complete without the child's drawing being displayed on its door. It is clear that when the child makes marks for him/her those marks have meaning and what we can see is how children attempt to collaborate with adults to ensure that it is understood that marks are meaningful. Children as mark makers make the meaning in the 'space between', that is, space between themselves and the readers of the marks. The readers of the marks in the case of the fridge are almost invariably close family members, most often the mother. In a way similar to how children learn to use language as an interactive process they do the same with marks and other representations. Just as when they use language they are active agents in the world so when they make marks they are positioning themselves in a very similar way.

We have stressed the meaningfulness of marks and suggested that this makes mark making analogous to language use but there are important differences that we need to recognize. In the first instance making a mark is a physical activity easily recognized by the maker and the viewer; just think about the push/pull movement needed to make even a simple line. In a way different from speech, marks have a physical permanence, something not always appreciated when they appear on the new wallpaper. So marks are always available, they are present whereas speech has always gone, it is past. The permanence of the mark allows theorists to generate accounts of the sequence of graphic development. Unlike speech there is no general common-sense knowledge of this; while all adults know language and recognize its structures, the same is not true of graphics. We shall now turn to theorists and theories that will enable you to understand the way that children represent experience and to recognize how important this process is in the development of thinking and communicating.

Semiotics

Semiotics at its simplest is the science of studying signs of all kinds, both linguistic signs, which may be spoken and written and all other kinds of signs, but especially visual ones. It is a controversial and often difficult field of study but we are going to use the insights of semiotics to help you understand and facilitate young children's graphic development.

Our discussion of the nature of signs draws directly on the pioneering work of the great linguist, Ferdinand Saussure. He made the point that words had meanings but that the word was arbiter. So in English the word 'dog' refers to and animal with four legs, a tail and a bark, but the French say 'chien' and the Germans 'hund'. Saussure overcame this apparent confusion, not by referring to words but by talking of signs. A sign can be thought of as having two parts, the signifier and the signified; it is only the putting together of the two that produces the sign. So the spoken word 'dog' in English when connected to what it signifies produces the meaning an animal that barks. The meaning then is in the signifier/signified relationship and that is almost always social. In the case of language we hardly ever use or want to use one signifier in isolation, so the total meaning arises from the way that the meaning of any word is bound up with those that precede and/or follow it. The same is often true of pictures and readily seen in films.

Our analogy with language may have put the emphasis in such a way that you assume that when children are making marks they are some how evolving a system that meets conventionality. In the case of language this is of course true, no matter how difficult it may be to make meaning transparent, and the struggle to do that uses established and recognized conventions. For all of us this struggle exists but for children they are not merely struggling to use conventions but both learning them and learning their use. The same cannot readily be said for graphic communication unless we accept that certain conventions must be used and are the apogee of representation. In the West, perspective has been taken as the ultimate goal of 'good' representation. This is often expressed in commonsense terms as the painter showing us exactly what we see, but as the cubists demonstrate, that is not the same as trying to represent what the painter sees. Although there is a considerable body of literature that argues that children's drawing is inevitably headed towards 'good' representation, we need to acknowledge that like the cubist they may be trying to represent their understanding of the world. This is somewhat different to a wide range of scholars who have treated children's mark making and drawing seriously. Hagen puts it this way:

> Many writers have offered descriptions of the stages in the development of drawing. . . . these writers vary a bit from one to the other but generally they all conclude that the child is supposed to go through [the four] stages of pictorialism or spatial representation. (Hagen 1985, p. 69)

Hagen's summary offers the following stages:

1. The complete absence of space or of objects alongside one another;
2. Conscious but unsuccessful attempts to represent space;
3. Successful but incomplete spatial representation, using perspective foreshortening;
4. Coherent pictorial representation where children take pains to use the laws of perspective.

These stages seem to set out the way in which children will create a conventional signifier that will lead to an unambiguous sign. Although Hagen summarizes so clearly the position of a large number of scholars, she is sceptical about the goal of children depicting faithfully what they see. The insights of Roland Barthes are significant here. In his seminal essay 'Rhetoric of the image' he makes the point that images/visual representations are at best ambiguous, they are open to a variety of possible meanings, but we endeavour to create a stable and unambiguous meaning by the use of language. You will have noticed how eager adults are to get children to label their drawings and maybe you have noticed how adults often create the label for the child. In doing this, the adult is attempting to fix the meaning, to validate the work of drawing, to place it into a conventional school programme.

Knowledge and understanding of the world and its representation

We have indicated that we are suspicious of the idea that children go through developmental stages leading to some form of conventionality, put crudely as the move from scribble to art. Rather than focusing on what children are not achieving we think it is important to treat seriously what children actually do and what meanings they are seeking to make.

Piaget, like the writers that Hagen critiques, views young children's drawing as ways of showing their underdeveloped power of understanding and of thinking. He describes young children's thinking as pre-operational, as not having any of the characteristics of logical thought; this is a stage on a journey to rationality. Even so he does not see children's drawings as being deficient in some way but rather he treats them semiotically. Young children's drawings are signifiers both of what actions they are taking in the world and of their cognitive processes. What we can say is that the drawings are both representing and constructing their own cognitive development. Many psychologists from a variety of theoretical perspectives have used children's drawings to help them describe how individual children think and in some cases how advanced or not that thinking is. This use of children's drawings ascribes meaning and significance to them from the perspective of the adult. Unlike the study of language development where it is now largely accepted that meaning cannot simply be defined by convention or the decision of an adult, children's drawings are treated as simple and unproblematic. You will have read in this book and in others that that is rarely the case.

Piaget was a pioneer in the study of children's cognition but his focus on thought as internalized action has rather reduced drawings to windows via which we can see children's thought. The important work of Athey (1990) and her colleagues, who draw on Piaget's insights, show us a different way of thinking about the development of thinking and how we might describe and interpret children's drawings. She is not interested in the use of drawings to establish the cognitive level at which the child is operating. Commenting on the work of Kellogg she accepts that Kellogg has shown that we can identify 20 basic scribbles and that these are culturally invariant. What she means by cultural invariance is that regardless of, 'ethnic, geographical and cultural influences young children the world over make identical scribblings between the ages of two and five years' (Kellogg 1968, p. 1). In accepting this Athey is demonstrating her adherence to the basic Piagetian principle that children the world over think and then develop cognition in the same way.

What is important for us is the way in which Athey deals with children's drawings/representations. Like Kellogg she treats them very seriously but seeks to show how 'children become able to represent known events symbolically' (Athey 1990, p. 40). What does this mean? It means that in play children can use objects to represent radically different things, for instance the upturned table may at various times be, a bus, a lifeboat or a removal van; so the table is a symbolic representation but as you will have noted it is not a stable symbol, and we only know what it is when the children tell us. This example is from play; if we look at drawings we can see the same thing happening. A child draws a series of parallel lines and we know what they mean when she announces they are pipes; she may attach a different meaning later in another conversation. Athey takes what used to be called pre-operational thinking and recasts it as the stage of symbolic functioning. She makes the bold claim that she can create this description because she deals with what the children do spontaneously and not what they do when adults try and get them to do. Critical to what Athey is arguing is that when adults work with children they can observe their actions and discuss their drawings. When they do that, which does not mean telling the children what to do, they can learn about children's abiding interests and that tells us what kinds of intellectual schema they are using and developing. So drawings show cognition; they not only represent thinking, but equally importantly show how they are thinking.

Earlier we referred to those who study children's drawings to demonstrate how they are stages on the road to efficient and also aesthetic representation. Athey takes a similar view that drawings can be used to demonstrate development but in her case cognitive development. The graphic schemas that children make represent their intellectual development. What is important here is the fact that Athey claims that intervention can facilitate development. These interventions should be planned on the basis of the children's abiding interests and schemas which are reflected in their drawings and play. Interventions involve conversation but go much beyond this. The children become fascinated by snails and their representation is of the shell as the spirals are the object of the children's curiosity. In order to facilitate development the children are put in the way of different forms of spirals in the world, toys from the toy box, more exciting a helter-skelter. In Athey's words, 'Schemas have been well nourished by wide experiences, consistently accompanied by articulate speech . . .' and development has been facilitated.

Activity

- Find out what you did habitually between the ages of, say, 2 and 5. Ask those who knew you whether you had a kind of obsession with certain objects and actions.
- Discuss this with others in your group and collectively come to some conclusion as to what schema or schemas you were developing.

Focusing on the social

Piaget and those who have developed his ideas stress the way in which action is the most important thing for a child's development. The organism is set up to develop physically and mentally and in the case of mental development the path is towards logical abstract reasoning. What is always at question is what the role of adults, the social context and language are in that development. Athey, whose routes are clearly in Piaget's work, stresses the importance of first hand experience and then articulate high quality adult talk. This combination she argues makes a sustained positive difference to children's intellectual development. This combination of speech and experience is very important in the work of Vygotsky and his colleagues. We will try to show you how, by using the insights of very different theorists, you can began to explore what the relationship is between children's mark making and the social world in which they live.

If we follow a Piagetian framework we would see the earliest marks as psycho-motor activities in which the push-pull actions are adapted by the use of a tool. The marks make available some sense of the sense the child is making of the world. Piaget argues that what is happening is that the child is both internalizing the action and representing it; the process of internalization is the way in which thought develops, and the representation to some extent shows that development. Athey's study begins by accepting that representation 'stems from action' but she goes beyond this. She makes a case for the way in which representation develops motor skills and that through these motor activities, more and more sophisticated actions can be conducted. These actions internalized are thought, if we follow the classic Piagetian argument. She goes beyond this by claiming that everyday stuff experienced by children is represented in some form of convention.

> [R]ight from the earliest representations, content had a perceptual equivalence to graphic form and there appeared to be a heightened perception of object in the environment that also matched existing form. Objects such as 'aeroplanes', 'fences' and 'scaffolding' were not represented with circular scribble but with grids. (Athey 1990, p. 93)

Activity

We are suggesting that children's graphic schema are both a way of representing the world and one of their tools for thinking. Look at Martha's drawing:

- Are there things about it that tell you that this is a very considered piece of work?
- Can you identify particular shapes she has used?
- Is it possible to speculate what the cognitive element of this drawing might be?

You will find Athey's book helpful in thinking about these issues.

Ideas of graphic schema as tools for thought, of perceptual equivalences that draw on cultural contexts, and of the cultural nature the resources children have access to, make for an overlap between a Piagetian and a Vygotskian framework. Athey's children draw on the culture available to them, it makes demands about what they should know and to some extent how they will represent that knowledge. The tools they can use are part of their cultural situation. They have readily available things such as pencils, crayons, paint and paper as well as a range other materials such as fabric, cardboard boxes of different shapes, squeezy bottles and a myriad of other things you will be familiar with. Using these kinds of tools to represent their environment changes the way they look at and think about their environment. We can say think about because of the way they make use of the tools. Luria (1994), Vygotsky's pupil and collaborator says

> the tools used by man not only radically change his conditions of existence, they even react on him in that they effect a change in him and his psychic condition. (Luria 1994, p. 46)

What we are stressing here is the social world in which the child lives and to which the child adapts. This process of adaptation is not simply to 'fit in' but is part of the process through which thinking develops. Thought with no expression is entirely self-centred and, more than that, is unlikely to expand and develop. Thought that finds expression comes into the social world and in so doing transforms the thought itself. The child's graphic representations lead to response by others, usually adults as we said earlier. These responses involve speech so the child begins to use speech alongside graphic representation. What we have is 'the naming of parts' by the child; this is where the Piagetian and Vygotskian interpretations part course. Athey in her careful analysis and description of children's representations and how they can be used to extend thinking shows how adults' spoken interactions with children are important but she does not show how speech and action together become thought. What we want you to think about is how the action of representing, the physical making, is internalized together with the word; they are one sign not two.

The child begins to represent something in drawing, then has a conversation with another and then 'labels' the drawing. This complex of language, action and drawing become one and then thought changes and thinking develops. What we are saying is that it is not the role of the adult to direct but to engage in meaningful conversation. Plotting the direction in which thought develops is extremely difficult and that development, according to Vygotsky, often defies logic in that the logical arrangements of thinking only comes after its development. The imposition of a logical sequence makes little sense and may even impede development. Nevertheless there always seems to be a commonsense desire to force logic upon children even though we are all well aware that logic is often absent from adult thinking and argument.

Perhaps more important is the fact that we cannot say that teaching children to make marks teaches them to think. None of the major theorists we have discussed would argue that you can teach children to think through teaching representation. You can, however, create circumstances under which they are better enabled to develop cognitively. It is obvious from our discussion so far that we are confident that the provision of representational tools and materials, the opportunities for children to pursue their abiding interests and for proper conversations for those around them are necessary but not sufficient means by which children's thinking can be enhanced.

Policy and practice

It is attractive to policy makers to think that they can simply import practices and policies from other settings where they have been successful. We have seen a number of instances in England of policy makers trying to simply import and impose other systems.

High/Scope

In the 1980s the system called 'High/Scope' an early years learning programme from the United States was pushed very hard by some policy makers as a solution to educational disadvantage. It failed to take root largely because of the assumption that it was politically and culturally neutral, or that English early years educators had no meaningful ideas of their own. It rapidly became a mantra, 'plan, do, review' – children were expected to choose and plan their activities first, documenting them in a planning book or on a chart. What it assumed was that the children had no ideas about what they wanted to do and that only the activities set out could be done and those were the only valuable activities. It left the children with no space to represents their own world or their own feelings. Currently there is wide spread advocacy of the Reggio Emilia early years system and its wholesale importation is undoubtedly attractive to some policy makers and to this we now turn.

Reggio Emilia

The much praised Italian system has received support from early years' educators and has been used as a reference point by central policy makers. It is seen as providing support for current policy but in fact this is a misreading of the curriculum and pedagogy used in Reggio Emilia. You may have read in discussions of the Reggio Emilia project of the many voices of children and have spotted the references to children's expressive, symbolic and cognitive languages. Hertzog (2001), for example, writes of graphic languages used to advance children's thinking and to present them with challenges. She says these languages help children communicate about and wrestle with their ideas and although she suggests some relatively simple practices that might be adopted she recognizes there is more to the approach than practicalities.

Since we have been talking about representation in a similar fashion it might be tempting to think we could just borrow the approach and advocate its use in England. A dialogic approach to pedagogical learning would certainly seem preferable to a bureaucratic one, whilst the involvement of local communities in the development of provision and the importance of engaging with children (through listening and observation) resonate with what we have been saying. Even so we would want to recognize, as do Kinney and Wharton (2008), the ground work that must necessarily be undertaken for a 'local Reggio' to emerge. The importance of observing and listening to children is an essential part of the Reggio approach, and it is used to inform the direction of learning. In England we have seen the way in which assessment directed from the centre has 'invaded' the space of the youngest children. It has been disguised as profiling but in effect this is a form of assessment since the profile is to be used by teachers to plan the programme for children both in reception and later classes. Pupils who have an incomplete profile need to complete it in order to be successful – this to us seems like remediation! This use of an example to support intervention has been the story of early years' policy making since the last days of the Conservative party's rule which ended in 1997.

We have argued above that young children are creative and can interpret and represent their world in their own way. In order to do this they need the space and freedom to do it. We have shown you how respected thinkers about the nurture and development of young children have stated that play is central to wholesome development, and that play is what is wholesome for the child. Policy makers, while appearing to agree on the necessity of play, have then sought through policy injunctions to define and organize that play, making it into an instrument of state pedagogy. Ruth Kelly as Secretary of State made great claims that when the new Early Years curriculum came on stream in September 2008 it would not be driven by assessment but by goals; you may well think that the only way to know if a goal has been met is to assess it. More recently Polly Curtis (2008) in *The Guardian* reported some changes which at first look like a retreat from a formal curriculum for the teaching of literacy but actually simply reserve the space for further intervention.

> The controversial new curriculum for under-fives, to be introduced from September, sets 69 learning goals for all children when they start school. A review is now being held into two goals: requiring four and five year olds to have a basic understanding of phonics and to be able to write their own names, form simple sentences and use basic punctuation.

The question is whether the current review of the curriculum will actually return the early years curriculum to the abiding interest of children, but that seems unlikely since the review is being led by the person who is convinced that the early imposition of formal literacy teaching is the right thing.

> Sir Jim Rose, who is reviewing the primary curriculum, will consider whether or not the goals should be changed. The minister released research which suggested that 46% of children already achieve the first of milestones and 30% achieve the second. (Curtis 2008)

Rather than accepting that young children learn naturally through play they distrust this idea and seek to impose 'order and system' on the child.

We have been arguing that children's representations – spoken, graphic and symbolic – jumbled together as they are in everyday life, are essential tools for learning. We have suggested that the graphical, verbal and experiential are interwoven with and by young learners. We have prioritized children's mark making in our discussion because it gives children the space to tell themselves and others about how they understand the world. A fairly simple reading of the Practice Guidance for the Early Years Foundation Stage seems to lead away from this perspective.

Look through the Practice Guidance for the Early Years Foundation Stage.

- What are children expected to enjoy and at what age?
- What does this tell you about the design of the curriculum?

We conducted an activity similar to that described above, looking for references in the guidance to marks and mark making. Since representational space is so important for children's purchase on the world you might expect to find references scattered throughout the document. Whilst this was not the case we can note that there are three references to marks and mark making in using equipment and materials and eight in exploring media and materials, none of these referred to children older than 50 months. The majority of references, 18, were found under writing with a further 4 references under handwriting, again up to 50 months old. Thus we have 22 references to marks and mark making related to writing and 11 related to creative development. This would appear to be a downward curriculum pressure where time for creativity is being stolen from children to press them into further literacy-related activity.

We leave it to William Wordsworth, who our policy makers seem to be ignorant of, to express out concern where he points out that children:

> … cometh from afar:
> Not in entire forgetfulness,
> And not in utter nakedness,
> But trailing clouds of glory do we come
> From God, who is our home:
> Heaven lies about us in our infancy!
> Shades of the prison-house begin to close
> Upon the growing Boy

Summary

- There has long been a recognition of the importance of the arts in early education, evidence of this can be found in the writings of the early 'great educators'.
- Theorists, often psychologists, have established clear links between young children's minds at work at their painting and drawing. It can be said that children are using graphic marks as signifiers of their meanings.
- When adults work with children and discuss their representations with them the adults learn about children's thinking and their abiding interests.
- Language and action become thought as children talk about their representations.
- Recent pedagogical initiatives continue to recognize the importance of children's painting and drawing for their intellectual development. Professionals will be wary of policy initiatves that reduce children's representational activity to 'pre-writing'.

Recommended Reading

Athey, C. (1990) *Extending Thought in Young Children: A Parent-Teacher Partnership*. London: Paul Chapman Publishing Ltd.
Brierly, M. (ed.) (1979) *Fundamentals in the First School*. London: Basil Blackwell.
Eisener, E. W. (1982) *Cognition and Curriculum: A Basis for Deciding What to Teach*. New York: Longman.

Bibliography

Arnheim, R. (1972) *Art and Visual Perception*. London: Faber & Faber.

Athey, C. (1990) *Extending Thought in Young children: A Parent-Teacher Partnership*. London: Paul Chapman Publishing Ltd.

Barthes, Roland (1964) Rhetoric of the image, in Barthes, R. (1985) *The Responsibility of Forms: Critical Essays on Music, Art and Representation*. Transl. Richard Howard. Berkeley: University of California Press.

Curtis, P. (2008) Early years writing lessons do no good, *The Guardian*, 14 July 2008.

Eng, H. (1931) *The Psychology of Children's Drawings*. London: Routledge and Kegan Paul.

Hagen, M. A. (1985) There is no development in art, in Freeman, N. H. and Cox, M. V. (eds) *Visual Order: The Nature and Development of Pictorial Representation*. Cambridge: Cambridge University Press.

Hertzog, Nancy B. (2001) Reflections and impressions from Reggio Emilia 'It's Not about Art!', *Early Childhood Research and Practice*, 3, 1. Available online at: http://ecrp.uiuc.edu/v3n1/hertzog.html

Goodenough, F. (1926) *Measurement of Intelligence in Drawings*. New York: World.

Goodnow, J. (1977) *Children's Drawing*. Oxford: Open Books.

Harris, D. B. (1963) *Children's Drawings as Measures of Intellectual Maturity, a Revision and Extension of the Goodenough Draw-a-Man Test*. New York: Harcourt, Brace & World.

Kellog, R. (1969) *Analyzing Children's Art*. Palo Alto, California: National Books.

Luria, A. (1994) The problem of the cultural behaviour of the child, in Van der Veer, R. and Valsiner, J. (eds) *The Vygotsky Reader*. Oxford: Blackwell.

Piaget, J. and Inhelder, B. (1956) *The Child's Conception of Space*. London: Routledge and Kegan Paul.

Saussure, F. de. (1977) *Course in General Linguistics*. London: Fontana/Collins.

Vygotsky, L .S. (1962) *Thought and Language*. London: Wiley and Sons.

Wordsworth, W. (1947 [1807]) The poetical works of William Wordsworth: Evening voluntaries, itinerary poems of 1833, poems of sentiment and reflection, sonnets dedicated to liberty and order, miscellaneous poems, inscriptions, selections from Chaucer, poems referring to the period of old age, epitaphes and elegiac pieces, Ode: Intimations of mortality. Volume 4. Oxford: Oxford University Press.

Where Do I Fit in? Children's Spaces and Places

Alison Bailey and Stephen Barnes

Despite government initiatives aimed at enriching childhood experiences, it seems that children's spatial freedom is more restricted than ever. Provision for children appears to be 'top down', based on adults' views of what children ought to do, of where they should play and of what is good for them. We would all agree that 'every child matters' but are we in the United Kingdom, at the beginning of the twenty-first century, ensuring that there is space for children to have a childhood? James et al. (1998) argue that everyday spaces are 'dedicated to the control and regulation of the child's body, and mind through regimes of discipline, learning, development, maturation and skill'. Without some freedom in spaces – the home, public space and institutional settings – we cannot expect to see children develop fully. Matthews and Limb (1999) go further and argue that children are 'marginalized as "outsiders" within society'.

Firstly, focusing largely on the United Kingdom, we consider the spaces and places accessible to children in the home, the public realm and in structured settings such as nurseries. In the second section of this chapter we explore the significance of spaces and places to the growth and development of young children and finally consider the design of spaces and places for children.

What spaces and places do children inhabit?

In Great Britain in Victorian times the adage, 'children should be seen and not heard' was frequently applied not only in public places but also in family and domestic settings.

If we think that children are excluded, or at least unwelcome, in a variety of settings, we might ask ourselves why? Public perception of children as either 'angels' or 'devils' (Valentine 1996) may play a part in the lack of freedom for children. The vulnerable child, rural or urban (angel), is idealized and forbidden to venture out alone by over protective parents. Noisy, playful children may be cast as 'devils' by adults intolerant of their activities. Public intolerance of children is well illustrated by the experience of the Jigsaw Nursery in Hampshire. In 2005 the nursery was advised by Fareham Borough Council to restrict children to only one hour's outside play per day following complaints from neighbours about noise.

Unsupervised play

The world of the child has shrunk dramatically over the past 30 years or so. According to the DCSF (Department for Children, Schools and Families) 'the average age at which children are allowed outside unsupervised has risen from around 7 years in the 1960s and 1970s to just over 8 years in the present day' (DCSF 2008, p. 10). Furthermore, figures presented by the Home Office and the Department for Education and Skills to the 'Good Childhood Inquiry', an independent investigation into young people's lives, show the restricted nature of children's movements.

> Two thirds (67%) of eight to ten year olds have never been to a shop or the park by themselves, along with a quarter (24%) of 11–15 year olds. A further third of eight to ten-year-olds have never played outside without an adult being present. (Bennett 2007, p. 4)

Although these figures relate to older children, it is apparent that younger children have even fewer opportunities for independent exploration and play. If children's experiences and movements are increasingly being limited, then their knowledge and understanding of the environment and their interactions with others in society will be inhibited.

The reasons for such restrictions may be real or perceived. Parents and carers have a difficult balance to achieve, between giving children greater freedom and trying to protect them from harm. Greater freedom allows children to develop strategies to cope with modern life and to develop social networks, to become 'streetwise' and risk aware. On the other hand, greater freedom means greater risk. The breakdown of family and neighbourhood networks means that children are not necessarily known in their community and the weakening of this safety net is a factor in the increasing fear of 'stranger danger'.

The prevailing cultural and social norms within any society will affect children's access to spaces. Cultural norms may include segregation by gender or religion and in some societies girls do not play outside the home at all. Social networks also play a part in children's use of public spaces; age, gender and ethnicity may also contribute.

In terms of gender differences, research has traditionally shown that boys have been given more freedom to explore their neighbourhoods than girls. Lester and Maudsley's report for Playday (2006), based on a sample of children under the age of 18 years old, found clear gender-based differences in terms of types of play preferences. Boys tend to like more active, competitive play with a risk and fear factor, while girls were found to be more passive, using imagination and role play and valuing interaction with friends more highly. Indeed, Pearson (2008) reports that boys need to be active and that it has been shown that boys' play-fighting, peaking around the age of 7 years, is a social activity and is not aggressive. Such play-fighting is the way that boys get to know each other. Pearson quotes Palmer, a former head teacher who says that, 'it is a biological necessity that boys run about, take risks, swing off things and compete with each other to develop properly. If they can't, a lot of them find it impossible to sit still.'

However, Matthews and Limb (1999) suggest that for young children, parents are moving towards less 'gender-differentiated child rearing'. This partly reflects the equal-opportunities and feminist movements of the 1970s where there was a positive move away from gender-stereotyping of toys and games given to boys and girls, but also shows the shrinking of children's worlds because of perceived and real dangers in the outside world.

An increase in road traffic in both urban and rural areas is also a major reason for the shrinking of children's spatial independence. RoSPA (2007) report that approximately 100 child pedestrians are killed annually on the roads. In addition, poor town planning has created towns with many areas dangerous for all pedestrians. The domination of motorized traffic in towns has meant that streets have become through-routes devoid of safe places for children to play.

Voce (2007) notes that of those polled in a survey commissioned by Play England, 71 per cent of adults played outside in the street or area close to their homes every day when they were children compared to 21 per cent of children today. Since 1999 local authorities have had more power to introduce 20 mph limits. Approximately, £50m has been allocated for the development of Home Zone schemes in England turning streets in residential areas into places for pedestrians and cyclists. Such schemes, however, do not eliminate the car but rather seek to modify the layout of the street so that the motorist shares the street with other road users. Although it is reported that, 'research published in 1996 shows that the number of accidents involving children reduced by 67% in 20 mph zones incorporating traffic calming measures' (DCSF 2008, p. 67), this may not be sufficient to encourage parents to allow their children more freedom to play out unsupervised.

Reflection

- Where did you play when you were a child? What were your play places?
- Who did you encounter/talk to when out playing?
- Were you always supervised by an adult?
- If you work with early years children, talk to them about the places where they play.
- Compare your own freedom as a 5-year-old child with that of a 5-year-old today and with someone of an older generation. What are the similarities and differences?

Organized play spaces

Where streets and lanes are not available for children's play, then open spaces, parks and playgrounds become even more important. Increasingly, informal open spaces are reducing in number and extent. There is greater pressure on land than ever before, making accessible space at a premium. Between 1997 and 2005 the density of new build housing increased by 60 per cent, thus reducing the amount of play space per child to only 2.3 square metres, a tenth of the minimum desirable (Beunderman et al. 2007). There is consequently growing pressure to build on brownfield sites and many previously accessible play areas such as wasteland and derelict sites are no longer available. Additionally, many Local Authorities have sold off school playing fields. Health and safety issues mean that farmers are unwilling and unable to allow children to play in farmyards and fields.

In addition, children do not have equal access to spaces and places. Socio-economic and cultural differences affect who has access to and engagement with certain places. As many as 58,000 children under the age of 2 in the United Kingdom live in homes two or more storeys above ground level. Of these, over 11,000 live on the fifth floor or above (Office for National Statistics 2001a). Such youngsters are physically unable to gain access to the outdoors without being accompanied by an adult or older child. As they mature, they will desire access to more space. You may wish to consider at what age they will be allowed to take themselves to play outside. How might this compare with children growing up with level access to a private garden? For these children, organized play spaces may be particularly important.

Although low income reduces spending options available, children should not be seen as consumers of space. In line with the UN Convention on the Rights of the Child, every child has a legitimate right of access to playable space. The Children's Play Council holds that:

> whatever the market may provide, children's essential, everyday play needs should be met by the planning and design of accessible, playable public space wherever children live. (Voce 2007, Foreword)

Indeed with children denied the freedom afforded to previous generations, many would argue that we have to supply them with spaces to play in relative safety. Hart (1992) suggests that this involves the provision of some kind of 'token space', often a playground, but that they otherwise have to fit into the 'alien environments of the adult world'. Similarly, more recent research supports this view: Beunderman et al. (2007) argue that we increasingly

> exclude and marginalise the young . . . children and young people have limited independence – both financially and spatially – and depend on shared spaces more than others. With trends in Britain pointing towards less outdoor play, increased parental anxiety and less tolerance for children and young people, the impact of an unwelcoming public realm on their health and well-being is becoming increasingly clear. (Beunderman et al. 2007)

A focus on play grounds is thus viewed by some as a failure: Lipman argues that, 'the focus on playgrounds is an admission of defeat – you have to look at the entire streetscape, the sort of spaces that everyone uses' (cited in Beunderman et al. 2007, p. 63). The location of such playgrounds is also crucial: to encourage independence, they must be accessible and situated near to where young children live.

However, it can be argued that playgrounds are relative 'oases of safety' for children (Ball 2002) since of all accidents to children annually, only 2 per cent occur on playgrounds. Rather than reducing the number and availability of play spaces perhaps we should be campaigning for a far greater share of Local Authority budgets to be targeted on play provision for children. This makes sense economically, socially and in terms of health and safety. RoSPA recognize that places where children play should be as safe as necessary, not as safe as possible since without some risk, children will not develop 'risk assessment' skills. Exposure to injury or witness of injury teaches children the consequences of their actions. We thus need to manage risks, not eliminate them.

The increase in the use of commercial play spaces, particularly in urban areas means that the ability to pay has also become an important factor in children's access to spaces. Playgrounds in pub gardens or indoor soft play centres and play zones can only be accessed by those with parents and carers able and prepared to pay for access, though McKendrick et al. (2000, p. 295) question whether the consumer is really the child or the parent. They suggest that perhaps such commercial playgrounds 'provide primarily for the needs of adults (for themselves and with respect to how they want their children to play) and to a lesser extent, for the needs of the children.'

Adults may feel that they are addressing the needs of their children by buying into such spaces, but you may consider to what extent they are salving their own consciences for limiting the time they allow their children to play 'out' and 'buying' themselves some quality time while the children are occupied.

Reflection

- Do you feel that there are places where young children are 'contained' for the convenience of adults?
- If young children were consulted on the provision of play spaces for them, what do you think they would prioritize?

Special places

Although many spaces and places are designed specifically for children, these are not necessarily the spaces and places which children would choose. There is a clear distinction between 'places for children' and 'children's places' (Rasmussen 2004).

Young children are opportunists, often making the most of spaces and places in an ad hoc way. You may have seen a child in an empty cardboard box imagine he is in a racing car or a powerboat. They may equally use a patch of scrub or a prize lawn as a football pitch. My own daughter, when aged 2 ½ years, found her way into the space beneath the pulpit in church one Sunday during the sermon, and called out that all her friends should come to play in her new secret house. Versatile spaces are important to a growing child. Children see places for what they can do in them, how they can use them, not for what they are, or as Gibson (1979) said, children view places for what they 'afford' the child, not for what they are.

Rasmussen's (2004) findings for children aged 5–12 years in Denmark show a range of children's chosen play spaces. For example, Anders, aged 8, describes a photograph showing a piece of land in the countryside. He describes in detail the features of the 'town', Bumbleby, which he and his friend Karl have created, pointing out his and Karl's houses and where they had previously built another house, now collapsed. This 'random plot of land' has special meaning and identity to Anders and his friends and Rasmussen notes that although the boys were not playing there when they described it to him, their 'earlier experiences seem to be alive in their narration' (Rasmussen 2004, p. 159). This aligns with Nordberg-Schultz's (1985) concept of places having a 'genius loci', a distinct spirit which cannot be seen but can be explained through feelings. A 7-year-old girl, Line, talks to Rasmussen of her home play space as including the courtyard outside her home, a flat in a block around the courtyard. Her favourite places within the courtyard are 'the tree for climbing' and a box covering electricity cables, both of which the adults forbid them climbing. The designated play spaces within the courtyard, the sand box, swing and slide are of little interest.

Philo (2000) defines spaces as 'settings for interaction' and places as 'specific sites of meaning'. The interactions which define spaces may be interactions with innate objects (e.g. the crawling child investigating stones, cracks, toys in its path) or social (e.g. children interact with other children or adults or pets). It is these actions and interactions (what we 'do' and what we 'experience') in spaces which imbue them with meaning.

What is the significance of spaces and places for shaping young children's growth and development?

Pre-birth

Our experiences in a range of spaces and places have a dramatic effect upon our cognitive, emotional and physical development. The space of the womb provides the foundation for our growth. Our very earliest experiences may have a profound effect on the way in which we understand and negotiate our way through life.

Riley (2003) explains:

> In the womb, the foetus has begun to learn actively; sounds and sensations are noted and remembered. The music tracks played to pregnant women soothe their babies more quickly after birth than other music. The voice of a baby's mother is conducted to her, albeit imperfectly, via the spinal column while she is still in utero. (Riley 2003, p. 4)

Sensory experiences pre-birth provide a bridge between the enclosed and secure space of the womb and the new, wider, post-birth world.

Babies

The sound of the mother's voice is a crucial link between these two worlds. The tradition of swaddling also shows an understanding of the baby's need for security and warmth and in many less economically developed countries babies are effectively swaddled for much of the day by the practice of being slung to their mothers throughout all her daily activities. By contrast, in the United Kingdom babies in their first few months spend much of their time in a crib or cot.

For their well-being and future development babies need to interpret their sensory experiences to build schemas with which to cope with their expanding world. The process of strategy building starts from their earliest days during which they learn about the world through all of their senses, each experience building on previous knowledge. Babies are explorers. Touching, feeling, tasting, smelling, hearing and seeing their way to discovery along uncharted paths, they initially define the micro-world around them.

Increasing mobility and freedom allow an expansion of the child's territory and spatial awareness. With increasing age and experience they are able to select and utilize a range of these strategies in order to tackle new situations, constructing and making sense of the world around them. This is consistent with Piaget's (1929) view that a child's conception of space evolves through several stages of cognitive development as he grows older. These sensory experiences will include interactions with the physical, environmental spaces which expand with the baby's increasing motor skills and mobility. Social relationships are a major part of these sensory experiences.

Babies learn very early on to signal their unease or discomfort to encourage adults to respond by moving them and dealing with their needs. In extreme cases of neglect babies have no choice, their cries going unanswered. The plight of children in some Romanian orphanages was made known to the world in the 1980s for example through the focus on 2 year olds confined to cots. Their limited opportunities for movement, their poor nutrition and a shortage of social interactions all contributed to a lack of physical and social development.

Montessori (1912) observed that:

> Adults admire their environment; they remember it and think about it – but a child absorbs it. The things he experiences are not just remembered; they form part of his soul. He incarnates in himself all in the world about him that his eyes see and his ears hear.

If you watch a baby exploring his fingers, a toddler minutely examining an object she has picked up between her thumb and forefinger or a 3 year old absorbed in play you may find yourself in agreement with Montessori's statement.

Toddlers

Once familiarity and security have been established toddlers set out to explore an ever-expanding world. Nutbrown (2007) describes a frequent feature of exploratory play, 'toddling and dumping' as being where the child moves between a known and secure location and person to a new location a few paces away. This process is frequently repeated and objects/toys are taken from a to b until the child feels secure in the 'new' place. You may have seen a toddler doing exactly this in your GP's waiting room or in an airport lounge, and you may well have been the new friend receiving building blocks and smiles. Such interaction with another person may also encourage language development in the naming of things. This constructivist learning process is the model which we utilize throughout our lives, moving from the known to the unknown, the familiar to the unfamiliar, assimilating and accommodating, and ultimately being able to postulate in abstraction.

Repeated interactions in familiar spaces help children to develop the confidence and skills to assimilate and accommodate new learning. Interaction with other children and with adults will allow early learners, through experimentation and scaffolding, to consolidate concepts of 'self' and 'other' and to construct meaning in these spaces.

In the United Kingdom, Sure Start, the Framework for all those with responsibility for the care and education of babies and children from birth to three years, aimed for better outcomes for children, parents and communities and recognized:

> That all children have from birth a need to develop learning through interaction with people and exploration of the world around them. For some children this development may be at risk because of difficulties with communication and interaction, cognition and learning, behavioural, emotional and social development or sensory and physical development. (DfES 2003, p. 4)

Learning within the environment is an interactive process in which children's experiences help to inform their development. Children need to be given progressively more freedom to explore as they grow and develop. Through exposure to a wide range of spaces and places they are able to adjust their understanding when placed in new environments. Many of these encounters, whether positive or negative, will be significant to their perception of the world. Some of these places will be regarded as 'special' and will impact on their development throughout the rest of their lives. Montessori (1912) believed that 'children build themselves from what they learn in the environment'.

Young children

Tizard and Hughes (1984) and Anning and Ring (2004) argue that for early years children, their sense of self in school or in childcare settings may be different from their sense of self at home because of the relationships, expectations and activities associated with each context. The concept of place attachment is relevant here. Spencer and Blades (1993, p. 368) summarize Chawla's (1992) work on place attachments in children,

> to concepts of bonding and of rootedness: these describe necessary aspects of the healthy development of the individual leading out from an initial secure home-base where nurturance is to be found, through a broadening circle of places as the child grows up.

Absence of such 'place-based support' may lead to psychological disturbance, as found, for example, in homeless children.

The shocking discovery of Elisabeth Fritzl and some of her children imprisoned in an Austrian basement has recently highlighted the effects of sensory deprivation on children. Those children imprisoned have been found to be developmentally retarded in comparison to their siblings who lived a more normal life above stairs. Such extreme examples highlight the significance of spaces and places to children's growth and development.

Early childhood environmental encounters are clearly of paramount significance in shaping secure, healthy and happy people able to participate fully in society. Place has an important role in the development of self-identity and self-awareness. In 1938, Dewey stated: 'It ought not to be necessary to say that experience does not occur in a vacuum. There are sources outside an individual which give rise to experience' (Dewey 1969, p. 39).

As Malaguzzi (1996) reminds us: 'children need the freedom to appreciate the infinite resources of their hands, their eyes and their ears, the resources of forms, materials, sounds and colours.' And hence when considering children's development, a healthy balance must be achieved between adult direction and children's independence. Bruce (1989) noted the importance of allowing children the space to act upon their own initiatives:

> keeping a balance between children's and adults' initiatives is difficult. There is a difference between adults intervening to help children, and adults interfering. There is also a difference between leaving children to do as they like and helping children to have initiative, develop their own ideas, and make choices and decisions. (Bruce 1987, p. 39)

In this chapter we have raised a major problem facing children in the twenty-first century; that their hands-on experience within a variety of environments and opportunities for unsupervised play are becoming constrained. Equally, the limitation on their 'freedom to roam', is inhibiting the opportunities for greater socialization. Dewey (1938) and Prescott (1979) recognized that healthy development can only take place through a range of experiences within a variety of environments. Bruner (2004, p. 39) emphasized the importance of play, play spaces and meaningful interactions with adults in the development of children's language. If environments restrict the range of experience too much, then the likelihood is that conceptually, linguistically, emotionally, physically and cognitively, children's growth will be limited. Children's self-esteem, confidence and awareness of others can only be enhanced by providing a rich variety of environmental and social encounters.

Huttenmoser et al. (1995) illustrate the benefits to 5 year olds of being able to play unsupervised in the neighbourhood. A comparison of two families showed that a child allowed more freedom had twice as many playmates and knew more adults in the neighbourhood than his counterpart who was only allowed to play outdoors when supervised by an adult. Such constraints on childhood freedom will prevent full development of strategies for coping with and overcoming problems and issues which will arise throughout their lives.

Moving forward – how do we design spaces and places for children?

Well-designed environments enhance the possibilities for children's development. Montessori almost a century ago understood the importance of well-planned spaces and resources for young children's learning. The values we transmit in determining the quality and appropriateness of spaces for children in and out of school may well have implications for generations to come, for as Olds (2000) reminds us, 'our designs shape children's beliefs about themselves and life. In a well designed area, children are engaged and feel secure.'

Educational settings

Until the mid-nineteenth century, children as young as 4 years old were in industrial employment in England and Wales. The population of what is now the United Kingdom was approximately 21 million and the countryside was relatively open. Freedom to roam for very young children within their home and local environment was considerable though often focused around daily tasks. Today much of this freedom has been eroded with the population of the United Kingdom nearer to 59 million (Office for National Statistics 2001b), school attendance compulsory for rising-5s and with many children in their earliest years spending much of their formative time in nursery settings.

Government policy has increasingly acknowledged the importance of education from birth to 19 years. A major emphasis has been on the provision of adequate space for young children to engage in constructive play and the recognition in the Primary National Strategy and the Early Years Foundation Stage of the critical importance of the physical environment in influencing learning.

> It (the physical environment) gives children clear messages about how we value them and how we value learning. It can be supportive of independent learning. Developing independent learning has far-reaching implications for the ways that teachers or practitioners and children interact, the tasks that are set, the responsibility that children take for their own learning and the opportunities teachers or practitioners plan for children to initiate and extend their own learning .One way to look at developing independence is to consider the ways that the physical environment can support learning. (DfES 2004, p. 56)

It is a requirement of the EYFS that nurseries and schools with Reception classes have access to an outdoor play area or should make arrangements for outdoor play at an appropriate location nearby. There now appears to be a national acceptance of the need to move beyond play areas being simply a tarmac area and, if lucky, a football field. This is accompanied by the recognition that trained play practitioners should be employed to 'support children's learning through planned play and extending and developing children's spontaneous play' (QCA 2001).

Reflection

Take a little while to consider the nursery schools/playschools/schools which you attended or have known.

- When were those schools built?
- What play spaces were available both indoors and outdoors.
- What opportunities were/are the children given for free play?

Frequently, the places and spaces designated for the use of children have been 'hand me downs' or have been constructed on the basis of institutionalized budgetary formulae. Most often these places are concerned with behaviour control and containment rather than on notions of positive educational development.

> Too often child care takes place in society's cast off spaces, church basements, converted warehouses. Even centres 'purpose built' for children are often designed with more of an eye to adult priorities than children's needs. (Community Playthings 2002, p. 2)

Designing new settings for children

In order to promote a firm design framework, key elements of children's needs should be incorporated into the design brief. These include the need for the spaces to be:

- Inviting and welcoming; to have various levels of stimulation
- Well defined; safe but not risk averse
- Flexible so there are open spaces and closed areas; simple and complex with freedom for exploration
- Accessible for all children
- Suitable for independent play and for socializing
- Memorable. (Adapted from Olds 2000)

When considering structured settings, it is heartening to note that there is a growing awareness of the need for children to have access to more flexible play spaces. 'In a well-planned environment children can learn through play to explore their ideas and experiences in new and imaginative ways (QCA 2001, p. 5).

A rich environment will support children's emotional well-being, stimulate their senses and challenge their motor-skills. This is borne out by recent research into children's learning and the workings of the brain which shows that 'unless we incorporate activities into our learning programmes which allow the learner to "experience and feel" the subject of our learning, then the learning is less likely to happen: you can't have the cognitive without the emotional' (Smith, A. 2000 in Cree 2006, p. 14).

Malaguzzi's ideas embodied in the pre-schools of Reggio Emilia, post-World War II, recognize the environment as the 'third teacher'. The rooms all open on to a central space, the piazza, designed to reflect the local architecture and to allow interaction and freedom to explore indoors and outside. In addition, the local community and culture is brought into the learning spaces through objects and activities. Ceppi and Zini (1998, p. 14) suggest that, 'contemporary reality can and should permeate the school, filtered by a cultural project of interpretation that serves as a membrane and interface.'

In the United Kingdom, where this philosophy is incorporated, the link between indoor and outdoor spaces tends to be through transitional verandah structures to the side of nursery and school buildings. Natural light filters in, resources, equipment and clothing are located in the areas in which they will be used and children are thus encouraged to move freely to the environment most suited to the activity in which they are engaged. This type of learning space facilitates a negotiated curriculum in the early years.

A number of schools and nurseries in the United Kingdom have initiated projects to give young children closer links with nature creating pleasant outdoor spaces with trees, grassed areas, play apparatus made from natural materials and wild areas which are increasingly attracting birds, insects and small animals. Even in inner city schools, with limited outdoor space, largely covered with tarmac, teachers, parents and children have worked to incorporate natural materials and wild areas. The 'Eat-a-Metre' project in Bristol so far has 47 primary schools encouraging children to grow some vegetables, even if the garden is only a raised bed made from a pile of old car tyres.

GreenStart, a health and education programme funded by Groundwork in the North East, England, works with parents and children from birth to five years to promote the value of the outdoors, and in its first few years has already found positive outcomes.

Learning through Landscapes, a national charity, has been campaigning since 1990 for better school play grounds for children in the United Kingdom and works with schools and early years settings to improve their outdoor spaces. A survey in 2003 of 700 schools and early years settings who have improved their outdoor spaces shows that:

- 75 per cent have seen improved pupil behaviour;
- 64 per cent have seen reductions in bullying;
- 65 per cent have seen attitudes towards learning improved;
- 84 per cent have seen better social interaction;
- 66 per cent say school grounds improvements have increased community/parental involvement. (Learning through Landscapes 2003)

> ## Reflection
>
> Look at some case studies where Learning through Landscapes has worked with early years settings to improve their outdoor spaces.
> www.ltl.org.uk/schools_and_settings/early_years/case-studies.htm
>
> - Consider how children have been consulted and to what extent their ideas have been incorporated.
> - Select a case study to discuss with a colleague.

Consulting children

However as adults, perhaps there is an intrinsic difficulty with planning spaces for children. As adults we differ from children in our 'ways of seeing' in terms of rhythm, scale and content. Adults' ideas of what children want spatially are often at a tangent to those spaces which children themselves desire. Research for Fair Play shows a fundamental difference between adults' and children's preferred spaces, adults liking spaces that are, 'safe, orderly and easily visible and children preferring spaces with disorder, cover and loose materials' (DCSF 2008, p. 11). In general, adults have been responsible for the design of environments for children and thus some key elements in the design process may be missing.

A language and dialogue needs to be developed which does not patronize, is not tokenistic and which allows children to express their views and to have these valued throughout the design process, for

> What we believe about children thus becomes a determining factor in defining their social and ethical identity, their rights and educational contexts offered them.
> (Rinaldi 2001, p. 115)

There are encouraging signs that this process is beginning, with, for example, the planned introduction in 2009, through the Play Strategy, of an indicator of what children think about their parks and play spaces in their local area.

When given the choice, children prefer to play outside. Hart (1992) found that young children in a small American town liked rivers, woods, fields, hills, sliding places, jumping places, climbing places. Elsley's (2004) research shows children in a disadvantaged urban area particularly valued the wild space beyond the immediate environment of the streets and shopping centre (the 'Danger Woods', the ruins of a castle, an old slag heap). Children want, and need, places for interaction and quiet areas for retreat. Clark and Moss's (2005) work with young children found that outdoor places for activities were favoured. McHale's (2006) interviews with early years children found similar results but gained a deeper understanding of why pupils perceive certain outdoor places as special or favourite. She noted that the chosen places showed children's, 'emotional attachment and the links made between places and experience' (McHale 2006, p. 15). For example,

> many pupils spoke fondly of social interaction with friends that occurred in these places . . . other themes arising were the connections between these spaces and experiences outside of this location, e.g. the sandpit was chosen by one pupil as it reminded him of his holidays. (ibid.)

A well-designed outdoor space for young children should incorporate natural materials, have secure boundaries, a wide range of potential activities, secret places where children can play safely but out of immediate sight of supervisors and a sufficient area of empty, flexible space. Where children do not have access to wild spaces on a daily basis, the incorporation of natural features and materials in structured settings are important design considerations. Research by Titman (1994) showed that poorly designed and maintained school playgrounds lower children's self-esteem.

It has been found that the natural environment reduces stress and Lieberman (1999) reports that incorporating the outdoors into the school's curriculum leads to higher achievement. In the nineteenth century, Friedrich Froebel was advocating that young children experience a range of environments in which they should interact with plants, animals and a range of activities to liberate their abilities and provide them with better opportunities.

Children were consulted in the design of the new nursery at UWE, Bristol and the chapter by Helen Butcher and Jane Andrews shows how their ideas were incorporated effectively in the design process.

Our final example shows how a small scale project can begin to encourage new ways of designing for and with children. The $5 \times 5 \times 5 =$ Creativity project based in Bath and North East Somerset, began in 2000 involving five local artists with five early years settings and five cultural centres, influenced by the creative approach to education of the pre-schools of Reggio Emilia. Space and light are two key principles used to create thinking space, giving young children space to dream. Children's ideas are incorporated in all of these projects, but this is exemplified particularly well in Three Ways School, Bath, for children with special needs. Lightwells and flooring were designed from children's drawings and a sensory space is planned which will allow pupils access to,

> a world of fantasy, far-removed from their day-to-day life and difficulties. The egg-shaped venue will have sensors which will pick up on pupils' movements and then alter the music, lights and other sensory stimuli. Head teacher Julie Dyer said: 'For a profoundly disabled child, with little or no control over their own body, to experience the thrill of running through a green forest would seem the stuff of fantasy.' (Three Ways School 2006)

Segregating children?

Having looked at the design of children's outdoor and indoor spaces we now turn to the idea, implicit in all of our discussion, that children's spaces are separate from adult spaces. At the start of this chapter we asked you to consider where you see children – where they are allowed and welcome – and suggested that there is still an element of segregation apparent in our use of spaces. Matthews (1995, p. 457) takes the idea of children being unwelcome in the public domain a step further, suggesting that:

> Playgrounds, no matter how novel and stimulating, are conceived by adults to isolate and contain children within public spaces and, in so doing, contribute to 'a process of childhood ghettoization'. (Matthews 1995, p. 457)

These views are shared by Ennew (1994, p. 127) and, more recently, by Elsley (2004, p. 156) who says that, 'modern day children inhabit "spaces within an adult-constructed world", outlawed from public spaces and effectively corralled within institutions specially designated for them such as schools.'

DEMOS commissioned by Play England, interviewed children between the ages of 6 and 18 years as part of a study to investigate their experiences of their local public spaces. A key finding was that, 'children (outside the places designed for them) are at the bottom of a user hierarchy of public space that seems to be unconsciously assumed across Britain' (Beunderman et al. 2007, p. 65). One of the key recommendations is that the greatest gains for children,

> lie outside the boundaries of dedicated play areas. The concept of playable space is powerful and asserts that play should be possible across the entire public realm (not just in playgrounds) and involve all generations (not just children). (Beunderman et al. 2007, p. 109)

This can only be achieved though embedding this concept as an integral part of street design and taking '*place-shaping*' seriously.

In addition, Dumouchel (2003) argues that before education was institiutionalized, children learned from landscapes, from their interaction with the everyday, and that we should give children the opportunity to discover and learn about '*their own nearby worlds*'. She argues that,

> place-based education is . . . an effort to help learners to make connections. If we as educators can help our students to feel connected to their homes, their communities and the natural worlds that surround them . . . then we will be taking the first step towards a caring citizenry that understands – and thus cares about and for – their places on the planet. (Dumouchel 2003, p. 2)

Positive early life experiences in secure spaces and places will give children the foundations to build on and the inner strength to draw upon as they move out into an ever widening world. We need to show children that we value them by allowing them access to spaces and places which include the beautiful and the natural. We must give them freedom to play in the wider community, and also, in consultation with children, design safe places where they can try risky things. We also recognize how children value interactions with others as they develop a sense of place. If children's play spaces are totally separated from real environments and too sanitized we cannot expect children to develop an understanding of and respect for the environment.

Understanding is the key to effective communication at all scales. Making space for childhood by encouraging children to develop such understanding through feeling valued in the home, in the public realm, in schools and nurseries, and thus in the nation and in the wider world, should be a priority from the early years.

We began by recognizing that age, road traffic, the built environment and perceived stranger danger all contributed to the separation of children from public spaces. We suggested that manufactured spaces cannot substitute for the spaces children can creatively occupy. We went on to argue that the availability of playable space has positive consequences for children's well being and that undue restrictions on their play space had negative consequences. We then discussed the provision of appropriate learning spaces for children, we recognized the importance of consulting them on the design of their settings and then concluded with the challenge of including playable spaces that children can appropriate into our built environment.

Summary

- There are many spaces from which children are excluded or unwelcome. This relates partly to current conceptions of childhood.
- Opportunities for unsupervised play have reduced significantly over time.
- Organized play spaces have become more important and offer safe places to play, although not all children have ready access to these spaces.
- Some argue that these spaces are often designed more for the convenience of adults than the requirements of children, that they limit children's play, and that they form part of the marginalization of children as a group.
- Children create special playable places which have meaning for them.
- Opportunities for babies and young children to explore appropriate spaces are essential for their successful growth and development.
- We need to focus on consulting *with* children to design creative and inspirational settings and spaces for children but we also need to address the segregation of children and move towards creating spaces for *all* members of society.

Recommended Reading

Beunderman, J., Hannon, C. and Bradwell, P. (2007) Seen and Heard: Reclaiming the public realm with children and young people, DEMOS [Online] Available at: http://demos.co.uk/publications/seenandheardreport

Curtis, D. and Carter, M. (2003) *Designs for Living and Learning: Transforming Early Childhood Environments*. St Paul, MN: Redleaf Press.

Elsley (2004) Children's experience of public space, *Children and Society*, 18, 2, 155–164.

Rasmussen, K. (2004) Places for children – children's places, *Childhood*, 11, 155–173.

Bibliography

Anning, A. and Ring, K. (2004) *Making Sense of Children's Drawing*. Maidenhead: Open University Press.

Ball, D. (2002) *Playgrounds – Risks, Benefits and Choices*. Contract Research Report No. 426/2002, Health and Safety Executive.

Bennett, Rosemary (2007) Children who have everything except freedom to play outside, *The Times*, 5 June 2007.

Beunderman, J., Hannon, C. and Bradwell, P. (2007) Seen and Heard: Reclaiming the public realm with children and young people, DEMOS [Online] Available at: http://demos.co.uk/publications/seen-andheardreport [Accessed 24 June 2008]

Bruce, T. (1987) *Early Childhood Education*. London: Hodder and Stoughton.

Bruner, J. (2004), Life as narrative, *Social Research*, 71, 3, 691–710.

Ceppi, G. and Zini, M. (eds) (1998) *Children, Spaces, Relations: Metaproject for an Environment for Young Children*. Reggio Emilia: Reggio Children and the Commune di Reggio Emilia.

Chawla, L. and Malone, K. (2003). Neighborhood quality in children's eyes, in P. Christensen and M. O'Brien (eds) *Children in the City* (pp. 118–141). London: Hawthorn Press.

Community Playthings (2002) *Spaces: Room Layout for Early Childhood Education*. Sussex: Community Products.

Clark, A. and Moss. P. (2005) *Listening to Young Children: The Mosaic Approach*. London: National Children's Bureau.

Cree, J. (2006) Emotional attachment, in *Primary Geographer*, 59, Spring, 14–16.

DCSF (2008) *Fair Play: A Consultation of the Fair Play Strategy*. Nottingham: DCSF publications.

Dewey, J. (1938) *Experience and Education* [first published1897]. New York: Macmillan.

DfES (2003) *Sure Start: An Introduction to the Framework: Birth to Three Matters* [online]. Available at: http://www.Sure Start.gov.uk/improvingquality/frameworks/birthtothreematters/ [Accessed 12 August 2008].

DfES (2004) *Primary National Strategy, Excellence and Enjoyment: Learning and Teaching in the Primary Years – Creating a Learning Culture: Conditions for Learning* [online]. Available at: http://www.standards.dfes.gov.uk/primary/publications/learning_and_teaching/1041163/ [Accessed 12 August 2008].

Dumouchel, D. (2003) *Learning from the Land: the Power of Place*. Seattle: New Horizons for Learning.

Elsley, S. (2004) Children's experience of public space, *Children and Society*, 18, 2, 155–164.

Ennew, J. (*1994) Street and Working Children: A Guide to Planning*. London: Save the Children.

Gibson, J. (1979) The ecological approach to visual perception, in Hart, R. (ed.) *Children's Experience of Place*. New York: Irvington Press.

Hart, R. (1992) *Children's Participation: From Tokenism to Citizenship*. Florence: UNICEF.

Huttenmoser, Marco and Meierhofer, M. (1995) Children and their living surroundings for the everyday life and development of children, *Children's Environments*, 12, 4, 1–17.

James, A., Jenks, C. and Prout, A. (1998) *Theorising Childhood*. New York: Teachers College Press.

Learning through Landscapes (2003) [online], Available at www.ltl.org.uk/about-us.htm [Accessed 25 July 2008].

Lester, S. and Maudsley, M (2006) *Play Naturally: A Review of Children's Natural Play*. Commission for Playday 2006 by the Children's Play Council, National Children's Bureau.

Lieberman, G. (1999) *Closing the Achievement Gap: Using the Environment as an Integrating Context for Learning*. San Diego: State Education and the Environment Roundtable.

Malaguzzi, L. (1996) The right to environment, in T. Filippini and V. Vecchi (eds) *The Hundred Languages of Children: The Exhibit*. Reggio Emilia: Reggio Children.

Matthews, H. (1995) Living on the edge: children as outsiders, *Tijdschrift voor Economische et Sociale Geografie*, 89, 123–202.

Matthews, H. and Limb, M. (1999) Defining an agenda for the geography of children: review and prospect, *Progress in Human Geography*, 23, 1, 61–90.

McHale, S. (2006) Valuing the outdoors, *Primary Geographer*, 61, 14–15.

McKendrick, J. H., Fielder, A. V. and Bradford, M. G. (2000) Kid customer? Commercialization of playspace and commodification of childhood, *Childhood* 7, 3, 295–315.

Montessori, M. (1912) *The Montessori Method*, New York: Frederick, A Stokes Company.

Nordberg-Schultz, C. (1985) *Genius Loci – Toward a Phenomenology of Architecture*. New York: Rizzoli.

Nutbrown, C. (2007) Conference notes: Early Years Conference: Children's Spaces, Children's Places Conference, Bath Spa University, 9 July 2007.

Office for National Statistics (2001a) Census 2001. Available at http://www.statistics.gov.uk/cci/nugget.asp?id=348

Office for National Statistics (2001b) Census 2001. Available at http://www.statistics.gov.uk/census2001/pyramids/pages/UK.asp

Olds, A. (2000) *Child Care Design Guide*. New York: McGraw-Hill.

Pearson, N. (2008) Boys will be boys, so don't teach them like girls. *Times 2*, 8 July 2008, 10.

Philo, C. (2000) The corner-stones of my world, *Childhood*, 7, 3, 243–256.

Piaget, J. (1929) *The Child's Conception of the World*. New York: Harcourt Brace.

Prescott, E. (1979) in Greenman, J. and Prescott, E. (1979) *Caring Spaces, Learning Places: Children's Environments That Work*. Canada: Monarch Books.

QCA (2001) Planning for learning in the Foundation Stage, QCA/01/799 [online]. Available at http://www.standards.dfes.gov.uk/primary/publications/foundation_stage/940409/ [Accessed July 2008]

Rasmussen, K. (2004) Places for children – children's places, *Childhood*, 11, 155–173.

Riley, J. (ed.) (2003) *Learning in the Early Years*. London: Paul Chapman.

Rinaldi, C. (2001) in Ceppi, G and Zini, M. (eds) (2001) *Children, Spaces, Relations: Metaproject for an Environment for Young Children*. Milan: Domus Academy.

RoSPA (2007) Play Safety: Open Spaces and Public Parks, Oxon., RoSPA [also available online at: rospa.com/playsafety/inspections/public_parks.htm]

Smith, A. (2000) *Accelerated Learning in Practice*. Stafford: Network Educational Press.

Spencer, C. and Blades, M. (1993) Children's understanding of places: the world at hand, *Geography*, 367–372.

Three Ways School (2006) [online]. Available at: http://www.threeways.bathnes.sch.uk/sensory_studio_appeal.html [Accessed 28 July 2008].

Titman, W. (1994) *Special Places, Special People: The Hidden Curriculum of the School Grounds*. Godalming, Surrey: World Wide Fund for Nature/Learning through Landscapes.

Tizard, B. and Hughes, M. (1984) *Children's Learning at Home and in School*. London: Fontana Press.

UK Statistics Authority (2001) [online at www.statistics.gov.uk].

Valentine, H. (1996) Angels and devils: moral landscapes of childhood, *Enviornment and Planning D: Society and Space*, 14, 581–599.

Voce, A. (2007) Foreword to Report: Play England for Playday 2007, ICM, Children's Play Council [online]. Available at: http://www.playengland.org.uk/resources/design-for-play.pdf [Accessed July 2008].

Index